SPIRITUAL LAWS
And
PRINCIPLES
Of the
KINGDOM

81 Spiritual Laws

Laws Of Power And The Miraculous

Laws Of Financial Prosperity And Money

Laws Of Angelic Operations

Laws Of Resurrection

Laws Of The Anointing

APOSTLE FREQUENCY REVELATOR

GLOBAL DESTINY PUBLISHING HOUSE

Copyright © 2017 Apostle Frequency Revelator.

All rights reserved. No part of this book may be reproduced, stored in a retrieval system or transmitted in any form or by any means, electronic or mechanical, photographic (photocopying), recording or otherwise, without the written permission of the copyright holder.

ISBN: 9781521758588

The author has made every effort to trace and acknowledge sources, resources and individuals. In the event that any images or information has been incorrectly attributed or credited, the author will be pleased to rectify these omissions at the earliest opportunity.

Scripture quotations are all taken from the Holy Bible, the New King James Version (Authorized Version). First published in 1611. Quoted from the KJV Classic Reference Bible, Copyright © 1983 by The Zondervan Corporation

Published by the Author © Global Destiny Publishing House,
No. 17, 5th Street, Sandton, South Africa

Website: www.globaldestinypublishers.co.za

Email: frequency.revelator@gmail.com

Phone: 0027622436745/ 0027785416006/0027797921646

Book layout and cover designed by Mako for Global Destiny Publishing House

OTHER BOOKS PUBLISHED BY APOSTLE FREQUENCY REVELATOR:

How to Become a Kingdom Millionaire

Deeper Revelations of the Anointing

The Realm of Power to Raise the Dead

How to Operate in the Realm of the Miraculous

The Realm of Glory

New Revelations of Faith

Unveiling the Mystery of Miracle Money

The Prophetic Dimension

The Realm of the Spirit: A Divine Revelation of the Supernatural Realm

The Prophetic Move of the Holy Spirit

The Ministry of Angels in the World Today

Throne Room Prayers: The Power of Praying in the Throne Room

7 Dimensions of the Supernatural Realm

Divine Rights and Privileges of a Believer

Keys to Unlocking the Supernatural

The Dynamics of God's Word

7 Realms of the Supernatural Dimension

The Revelation of Jesus Christ

7 Supernatural Dimensions of Financial Prosperity

Spiritual Laws and Principles of the Kingdom

Rain of Revelations Daily Devotional Concordance

DEDICATION

This publication remains an exclusive property of Heaven as it has been given birth to by the Holy Ghost in the Throne Room of Heaven. As a product of the fresh breath of God released in the deepest territories of the glory realm, it is geared at propagating deeper revelations of God's Word, Divine presence of the Holy Spirit and Glory from the Throne Room to the extreme ends of the World. Therefore, this book is dedicated to millions of believers, whom through these revelations, shall move and function in higher realms of the Spirit, to the glory of God the father!

ACKNOWLEDGEMENT

This insightful, refreshing, profound and biblically sound revelation awakens the believer to the reality of the divine laws and principles of the Kingdom of God. It is chiefly the Holy Ghost who trained me in matters of operating in the deeper realms of the Spirit, hence it is my passion that the reader will see Him throughout the pages of this book and not any man. I would like to express my deepest and most heartfelt gratitude to my most beautiful and adorable wife Delight Nokuthaba Mpofu who is the love of my life, my life coach and business partner, for having supported me in every way in my ministry as a renowned global author. She is indeed such an amazing blessing that I will forever be grateful to have received from God. I owe a special gratitude specifically to one of my best spiritual sons, Paramjeet Singh Makani from the nation of India, who inspires me a lot through the demonstration of undefinable, uncharted and unrecorded miracles, signs and wonders in this very hour.

I would like to extend my gratitude to my ministry partners for creating such a conducive platform and spiritual climate for me to move in greater depths, higher realms and deeper dimensions of the anointing to shake the nations and touch multitudes around the globe. It is for such a reason that I have been used by God as a vehicle to propagate the new waves of God's anointing to the furthest territories across the globe, to accomplish God's divine plans at such a time as this. Allow me to extend a hand of appreciation to Great men and women of God all around the world who have been an inspiration to me: Dr Yana Johnson (London), Prophetess Nomsa M. Maida of New Breed ministry, Apostle Chris Lord Hills of the Supernatural

Church, Dr Franklin (South Africa), Prophet Mathew B. Nuek (Malaysia), Prophetess Menezes (USA) and Prophet Samuel Njagi (Kenya), for being instrumental in creating a conducive spiritual climate for the birthing forth of the revelations which God has laid in my spirit. Words fail to capture the gratitude I have for my own staff at *Global Destiny Publishing House* (GDP House), who have typified a new type of man coming forth on the earth, rising beyond the confines and dictates of the realm of time, to access higher realms of the Spirit: Further thanks goes to my ministry partners all over the world who have supported me tremendously by demonstrating an unquestionable thirst, perennial hunger and an insatiable appetite to read my books. I command the blessings of the Lord to abundantly marinate every sphere of your life with the rain of the anointing in Jesus Name! Further thanks goes to my siblings namely, Caspa, Kaizer, Taa, Keeper, Colleter and Presence Nkomo for their love and support in every way.

-Apostle Frequency Revelator

CONTENTS

Dedication	v
Acknowledgement	vi
1. Key Spiritual Laws & Principles Governing How To Operate In The Realm Of The Miraculous	10
2. Spiritual Laws And Principles Of Prosperity	38
3. Spiritual Laws Of Resurrection & The Raising Of The Dead	78
4. Spiritual Laws And Principles Of Operating In The Realm Of Anointing	88
5. Spiritual Laws And Principles That Provoke Miracle Money Into Manifestation In The Natural Realm	103
6. The Higher Laws Of Financial Prosperity	116
7. Spiritual Laws Governing The Operation And Manifestations Of Angels	132
8. Author's Profile	155

CHAPTER ONE

KEY SPIRITUAL LAWS & PRINCIPLES GOVERNING HOW TO OPERATE IN THE REALM OF THE MIRACULOUS

It is worth exploring the divine truth that there are laws and principles that God has put in place by which He governs the universe. These are categorically *physical laws* which govern the natural realm and *spiritual laws* which govern the realm of the spirit. For example, there is a law of gravity which stipulates that if you throw an object up in the air, it will evidently crash back onto the earth; the law of floatation which allows ships and boats to float on water, the law of aerodynamics that enables aeroplanes to fly and the law of electricity which helps us generate heat and light energy. The reality is that when we operate in obedience to these physical laws within nature, we reap positive results but when we violate them, the repercussions are severe. However, as much as there are physical laws, there are also spiritual laws which are the highest class of laws governing and controlling the entire universe. In the spiritual realm, God has established a court system with laws, principles and divine protocols which functions just like the court system of the natural realm.

Apostle Frequency Revelator

Just like physical laws, when we corporate with these spiritual laws, we reap alarming results but when we violate them, we face the consequences. It's a pity that most people do not understand the operation of these divine laws and protocols, which explains why the devil ends taking advantage of their ignorance, thus gaining a legal foothold that grants him the right to ensnare them into debilitating circumstances of poverty, sickness and defeat. There are certain principles that one can tap into in order to walk into the deeper realities of God's power. Just like there are laws of gravity which governs how to operate in the natural realm, there are also spiritual laws that govern the spirit realm or how to operate in the realm of the miraculous. These laws of the supernatural complement each other and are progressions to enter into the greater depths of God. Each of these laws has a specific manifestation that produces something special. However, it is unfortunate that many believers are failing to operate in the realm of the miraculous because they do not understand spiritual laws and principles which they could take advantage of to generate positive results. Spiritual laws and principles are therefore vital keys that unlock the doors into the supernatural and accentuate an avenue through which the power of God can flow.

It is a typical scenario in the body of Christ that so many people have the power but they do not know how to release it. Having the power is one thing and knowing how to tap into the realm of God to release that power is a completely different reality. In the church of Jesus Christ today, God has invested upon believers' tremendous, overwhelming and explosive power and authority but that power is not released as it should because of lack of understanding of spiritual laws and principles governing the realm of the spirit. They have the *exousia* power but they are not realizing how to tap, activate and exercise it. Failure to tap into the realm of power is what is allowing their homes to be plundered by the enemy without taking authority against it just like Adam allowed the serpent to tempt Eve and deceive her in his presence. It has been noted that a lot of Christians are allowing Satan to dominate their lives and wreak havoc in their families while they are busy crying to God like Moses facing the Red Sea, "Oh, *God, help!.*" But God is asking them, "*What are you doing with the power and authority that I gave you? Put to practice the principles which I have given you in the my Word and your way will open up!* Learning how to tap into the set spiritual laws and principles is therefore vital in birthing forth supernatural manifestations of God's power. You are definitely guaranteed to launch into the greater depths of the miraculous if these spiritual laws and principles are correctly applied, practised and activated.

LAWS OF POWER

A DEVINE REVELATION OF 21 (TWENTY ONE) FUNDAMENTAL PRINCIPLES OF DEMONSTRATING GOD'S POWER IN THE SUPERNATURAL REALM

1. *The Law of Impartation*

It must be understood that the power of God, His blessings and gifts flows through impartation and this is the reason why Paul pleaded with the Corinthians in Romans 1:11 that, *"Brethren I long to see you that I may impart a spiritual gifts so that at the end you may be established"*. There are different types of impartations. For example, there is *angelic impartation,* whereby angels imparts spiritual substances upon people during ministerial sessions, then there is an *apostolic and prophetic impartation* whereby man receive messages directly from God and then there is a *divine impartation* whereby divine substances such as the anointing, spiritual gifts and glory are imparted upon vessels. The greater truth is that spiritual things are received through impartation. The anointing is an impartation. Revelation is an impartation. Other spiritual substances like faith, wisdom, gifts of the spirits, and the power of God flows through impartation.

There are two ways through which an impartation of God's power or blessings is given, that is by loosing the blessing directly upon the recipient in the case of a supernatural visitation or divine encounter with God or by transferring the power or blessings from one person to the other .There are certain things which people cannot receive directly from God due to the degree of sacrifice and price to be paid for one to qualify to release those things. However, such blessings can be received directly from other men of God though *impartation*. Impartation from one person to the other takes place in three main ways, that is, through *atmosphere, association and influence. Impartation through atmosphere* implies that by virtue of coming under a spiritual covering where the atmosphere is already pregnant with the power of God, one can easily receive the power. *Impartation by association* implies that by virtue of developing partnership networks or relationship with a man of God who is anointed, the power of God can easily flow from him into a recipient.

Impartation by influence implies that by virtue of authority, power can be easily transferred or flow from a minister to recipients or those people to whom he preaches to. Therefore, as part of impartation, a minister could stir up or activates the gifts of the spirit in masses. In Numbers 27:18, God said to Moses, "*Take thee Joshua the son of Nun, a man in who is a spirit and lay thy hand upon him*". Why did God command Moses to lay his hand upon Joshua? It's because he wanted Joshua to receive an impartation of the *Leadership anointing* to take over from where Moses had left. This is to tell you that even blessings are transferred from one generation to the next through *the law of impartation*.

2. *The Law of Release*

The law of release is such a powerful divine prophetic principle which when tapped into, can result in an avalanche of God's power, blessings and anointing from the realm of the spirit into the natural realm. Do you remember when God declared in Zechariah 10:1 that, "*Ask for rain in the time of the latter rain and I shall give you showers of abundant rain*"? This is the essence of the *law of release*. Rain speaks of the anointing and in the context of supernatural power, this implies that if you need an unprecedented flow or avalanche of God's power, you must release it during the right time when the power of God is moving or flowing. This spiritual law awakens us to the consciousness that it is advisable to release God's supernatural power when people are ready to receive or when the spiritual atmosphere is conducive enough to unleash or release the power of God. Hence, there are two critical prerequisites for the release of God's power and that is; the extent to which the atmosphere and spiritual climate is pregnant with the possibilities of God and the extent to which people are ready to receive from God. The Bible further declares in Ecclesiastics 11:3 that *when clouds are full of rain, they empty themselves on earth*. Knowing when to release the power is one such a vital key to the flow of God's power. That is why Paul advises in 1 Timothy 5:22 that *no one must not be quick to lay hands* because at times the anointing might be building up like a cloud or accumulating until a particular point. Making haste to release the power under such circumstances might not produce expected results. The expectancy level of people somehow is a determining factor to the law of release. You only release the power when your faith level and expectancy levels of people are high.

This implies that we cannot declare the word if we don't have foreknowledge of what will happen. For example, if you are going to speak to a blind person yet you don't expect his sight to return, then rather don't say anything and

Spiritual Laws & Principles of The Kingdom

if you are going to tell the lame to stand up yet you don't expect anything to happen, you rather not say anything at all. Apostolic revelation breaks new ground by declaring what the father is saying and doing at this moment in time. This causes the Heavens to loose what God has authorised for the earth. When the Holy Spirit reveals something through the apostles and prophets, Heaven can no longer contain it, it must be released. However, the greatest challenge facing the Body of Christ is that Heavens are pregnant with the possibilities of God and is therefore ready to unleash from the womb of the Spirit the power, anointing and glory but the earth is not ready to receive or incubate that which Heaven has given birth to in the spirit realm. That is why in some cases, there is so much power that is released from Heaven but it never gets to be utilised effectively because people are not sensitive to the move of God. This is contrary to the will of God because Jesus declared in Mathew 18:18 that, *"Whatever we bind on earth shall be bound in heaven and whatever we release on earth shall be released in Heaven"*. This means as far as God is concerned, Heaven and earth are supposed to function in synchronisation, in order to release the blessings of God. It is God's ultimate plan that Heaven and earth work together as one and not as separate entities. If you understand the law of release, you will know when to ask and when your blessing has arrived after praying for it. The danger is that so many believers are praying and praying but they never get to know when their prayers have been answered or when their blessings have been released. The truth is that *release* and *reception* takes place concurrently. In other words, blessings are received from Heaven the instant they are released into the natural realm. Contrary to how the lukewarm church has portrayed, you don't release the blessings or power of God today and then wait for tomorrow in order to see the results. Instead, you must procure the blessings at that very time when you release them. With this understanding, you certainly realise that blessings manifests at the point of release, hence there is no need for waiting and procrastination.

3. *The Law of Response*

The law of response is such a powerful divine principle that precedes the law of release because in prophetic language, you can only respond to something that has been released. Do you remember when God declared in Jeremiah 33:3 that, *"Call unto me and I will answer thee and show you great and mighty things which you knewest not"*. This is the essence of the *law of response*. This law gives a practical guide on how to respond to the anointing, presence and glory of God when administered from Heaven. It states that in order to activate or harness God's power from the supernatural realm and precipitates it into the natural realm; you must be in a position to respond accordingly when you sense its presence in the atmosphere. In other words, your spirit must be in an upper room position to respond to what God is appropriating in the spirit realm. Whenever the presence of God shows up, there are always three types of people who would usually respond in a particular way under normal circumstances. Firstly, there are those who are *spectators*, and have no clue of what God is doing in the spirit realm, hence they don't take any notice of His presence. Secondly, there are those who are *resistors* and are able to sense the presence of God but they are simply resisting it because their spirit is closed. Thirdly, there are those who are *detectors* and are able to feel the presence and desire to participate in it but have no revelation of how to channel the presence or benefit from it. The word of God gives an account in Luke 5:17 of how *the power of the Lord was present to heal*. In other words, the atmosphere was charged with God's presence but nothing happened until four men took a leap of faith and lowered a bedridden man through the roof and he was the first to receive his healing. However, there are those who are *partakers,* who have received a revelation of how to respond quickly whenever they sense the presence of God. And notable is the realisation that it is this last group that always excels in matters of demonstrating the power of God. This is akin to the incident in Mark 9:20, whereby people were pressing upon Jesus but only one woman who had a flow of blood for twelve years knew the art of how to respond to the anointing and sneaked her way through to touch the hem of Jesus' garment and she instantly received her healing.

It is a typical scenario in many churches that God's presence is felt but nothing more happens. His presence is there because some people paid a price for it but now that it comes, no one knows precisely how to respond or how to act whenever confronted by the presence. The atmosphere remains charged yet no one actively participates in it. This culminates in a scenario whereby miracles, signs and wonders and transformations are delayed because people have no idea of how to respond and appropriate the blessings of God. It is wrong to find some people being spectators in the presence of God because God demands that he who comes in His presence must participate in order to reap benefits of power and blessings from it. The power of God meets every need depending on individual desire and while others are receiving deliverance, others are being healed and others receive breakthroughs and impartation of spiritual substances. Hence, the correct prayer that we should pray whenever the presence of God shows up is *"Lord, reveal the purpose of your presence"*. This is because whenever God show up, He comes for a specific purpose and what He wants to do today might be different from what He did yesterday. We therefore need to respond to the presence of God through elevated worship, prophetic declaration and proclamation of our blessings, shouting for victory, dancing and yelling in praise as well as through practical demonstration and exercise of the gifts of the spirit.

4. The Law of expectation

The expectancy level is such a powerful key that can provoke the power of God into manifestation. The Bible says in Acts 3:5, that when Peter and John came across a crippled man at the Beautiful gate of the temple, he gave them attention expecting to receive something and that is the reason why he received his healing on that day. In fact, every day, they had passed by that man on their way to the temple and this was not the first time. But on that day, the man was in a better position to believe. Sometimes, when you remain in an atmosphere of faith, your faith grows until you are expectant enough to receive. Likewise, on that day he passed by the Beautiful gate, Peter sensed that the man was expectant and rightly positioned in the spirit to receive, hence he healed him. The truth is that regardless of the level of anointing upon a vessel, no one can give you what you are not ready to receive. As a believer, you must expect to receive a miracle whenever you get to a place where the presence of God is moving. Unfortunately, there are certain preachers who struggle to help even their own congregation because they themselves lack genuine expectancy. A high level of expectancy places a demand on the anointing and produces tremendous results of power. Miracles tend to intensify when the expectancy level is high. The law of expectation is such a powerful divine principle in that miracles do not happen where they are needed but they occur where they are expected. The higher the level of expectation, the greater the dimension of miracles, signs and wonders.

There is however an intricate connection between *expectancy level* and the *law of response*. For example, to respond to the power of God, we need to expect something supernatural to happen. If we do not expect anything, then we will be unable to respond when there is a manifestation of God's power. God is extending His hand to give us the supernatural but we also have to extend our hands in return to receive it. The reason why God demands in Exodus 23:15 that *no man should come into His presence empty handed* is because He knows that if you come empty handed, you will not expect to receive anything from Him, hence He challenges you to bring something so as to stir up your faith level.

In a ministerial context, as you minister, you must watch the response of the people because how the congregation responds is vital for the smooth flow of God's power. Stirring up their readiness can be done in different ways, for example by declaring *"Are you ready for the power of the Holy Ghost?"* How they respond will tell you whether they are really ready and rightly positioned in the sprit to receive or not. Keep declaring that if there is anyone on wheel chair, there must stand up; if there is any blind person, their eyes will open up and if there are any people who are on the verge of death on sick beds, declare that they will come back to life. As you declare these words, the expectancy level will provoke faith in their spirits such that some will even begin to rise up without you touching them. This is the power behind the *law of expectation.*

Prophetically speaking, the glory of God is hovering over the church and it's starting to unravel in this end time season. In the same way a famer is expecting the seed he planted in the soil to bring forth fruits, everything within me is leaping in excitement as I sense a shifting in the atmosphere. The Holy Ghost is about to explode in the demonstration of signs and wonders that will ruffle the feathers of those comfortable with the status quo. There has never been a time like now when Heaven is so aligned with the earth as it is now. You can smell it in the very atmosphere. There is expectancy in the air that corresponds to the Heavens for what God wants to do on earth. The spiritual atmosphere is full of expectation right now. Like a pregnant woman expecting the imminent delivery of her baby, the womb of the spirit is pregnant and ready for the birth of something new. Expectancy is the breeding ground for miracles, signs and wonders. When you are expectant, Heavens releases a corresponding divine energy or supernatural influence to bring that which you expect into manifestation in the natural realm.

5. *The Law of receptivity*

The law of receptivity is such an important divine principle in matters of operating in the realm of the miraculous because it is what determines how much power or anointing a man can receive from God. In Mark 8:27-30, Jesus once asked His disciples a simple question," *Who do people say that I am?*" This is the essence of the *law of reception.* The reason why Jesus asked His disciples this rhetoric question is not because He wanted to know how popular He was. Instead, it's because He wanted to establish how people received Him because how people receive you as a minister determines the effectiveness of the message you preach to them. Moreover, your ability or capacity to receive from God will automatically determine how much of His blessings can be imparted into your spirit. It is unfortunate that many believers tend to overemphasise the idea of giving buy they never focus on how to receive. This is because receiving is as equally important as giving. If you only know how to give but you don't know how to receive you will find yourself losing more but never gaining anything. It is a typical scenario in the body of Christ that many people are eager to stand and participate in the presence of God but the greatest challenge is that they do not know how to receive from the presence of God. In some cases, while the spirit of God is moving and imparting the anointing and other spiritual substances, people are also busy praying and preoccupied with their own agendas and programs and in the process, they are not able to receive what the Spirit of God is appropriating in the meeting. Some people do not receive because their conductivity level is low, meaning that they are poor conductors of the power of God while others are good conductors of the same power.

Some people do not receive because their spirits are closed. The power of God is flowing but their spirits are closed. On the other hand, others are able to receive because they are rightly positioned in the spirit to receive. Some people do not receive because they are in the realm of flesh and not in the spirit and they tend to conceptualise how to receive from a carnal perspective. The Bible declares in John 3:27 *that a man cannot receive anything unless it is given from above*. The extent to which one's spirit is activated or developed will determine how much he will receive from God. That is why spiritual exercises such as prayer and fasting opens and aligns our spirits and makes it easy to receive from God.

6. *The law of expression*

Knowing how to express your spirit in God's presence without shame, fear, hesitation or unbelief is such a key determinant to partaking of His glorious power and blessings. Expression in this regard entails developing a high level of *sensitivity, acknowledgment and consciousness of God's power*. Some people are not able to appropriate their blessing because they are not *sensitive* to the move of the spirit. In other words, they cannot sense or detect the presence due to the fact their spiritual senses have not yet been activated, developed or trained to operate in the spirit realm. Moreover, some people do not receive because they are not *conscious* or cannot discern God's presence. Developing one's level of consciousness through spending time in the presence of God is one such vital key to receiving or flowing in the power of God. *Acknowledgment* of the anointing or the power of God present is also a highly imperative action.

The Bible records in Mathew 20:29-34, that *when the blind man heard that Jesus was passing by, he cried out loud* and because of his high level of expression, Jesus healed him. According to the culture of the people at that time, it was a taboo for a man in his sins to cry out to a Rabaai but because of his desire to reach out to God, the man expressed himself vocally until Jesus paid attention to his cry and healed him. The scripture further proclaims in Genesis 18:1, that *when Abraham saw three angels purporting to be passing by, he ran after them and invited them to come to his house* and because of his expression, he was blessed at the end. All these are physical expressions but there are also different ways of expressing one's self in the spirit and that is through praying in other tongues, laughing and singing in the spirit, dancing in the spirit, travailing in prayer, falling under the power and how one expresses himself will determine the amount of power that will flow through him

It is evident that other people try to resist or stop the flow of spiritual expressions and in the process they short circuit or deactivate the power of God. For example, the Bible records a myriad of incidents where men of God expressed themselves fully before God. For instance, David danced in the presence of the Lord until his clothes were torn, the apostles were so drunk in the spirit on the day of Pentecost to the extent that they were out of control, Saul prophesied until he tore his clothes off although this manifestation ended up being in the flesh. These were such powerful expressions that launched them into greater depths in the spirit. However, while in the presence of God, some people tend to maintain their cool and be overly conscious of their self and in the process they fail to express themselves, hence receive nothing from God. It is therefore advisable that you release yourself unreservedly in the presence of God because the extent to which your spirit is open will determine how much you can receive from God.

7. *The Law of Connection*

It is a greater truth that the power of God and His blessings, anointing or glory flows through divine connection. Jesus declared in John 15:13-17 that, *"I am the vine and you are the braches grafted in the vive, therefore abide in me and I shall abide in you.* This implies that if you stay connected to God, His divine power will continuously flow upon your life and the opposite is true. Do you know that when the Bible says in Psalms 91:1 that *He that dwells in the secret place shall abide by the shadow of the almighty*, it actually speak of divine connection? This fruits or results of such divine connection are protection, prosperity, promotion, increase and so forth. Therefore, continuously staying in the presence of God will also ensure that you draw from the source of power.

However, the power does not only flow when you are connected to God but when you are connected to those upon whom the Lord has made an investment of His power. Our blessings and destiny are closely related with those to whom God has connected you. God will connect you to specific people, hence we must be a wise discerner of relationships. It is through relationships that we capture the mantles and blessings upon those whom God has connected us. On the other hand, if you disconnect yourself from a spiritual covering, you lose the anointing because one would have been cut off from the atmosphere, association and influence, in the same way a branch is cut off from a tree. However, some divine relationships are under heavy attack because whenever God connects us to someone, Satan will try to destroy the relationship because he knows that if we never make such a connection, our purpose will never be completed. Therefore, if you want to launch into greater depths of the miraculous, connect yourself to a source of power and miracles, signs and wonders will follow you.

The law of connection also implies being at the right place, at the right time, doing the right thing. The law of connection entails connecting yourself to two fundamental sources of power, that is, *connection to God* and *connection to His word*. Connecting one's self to the word of God is tantamount to connecting yourself to God because He has placed His word above His name. Hence, you are guaranteed of *kratos power* that is leased from the pages of the Bible straight into your spirit when you meditate on the word of God. Do you remember that the Bible declares in Psalms 1:1-6, that *blessed is a man who walks not in the counsel of the ungodly, nor stand in the seat of the scornful but his delight is in the law of the Lord and upon it he meditates day and night. He shall be like a tree planted by many rivers, whatever he does prospers.* Do you notice that prosperity is conditional; in other words it is dependent on the extent to which you mediate on the word of God? This is the essence of *connection*. The above scripture unveils the reality that prosperity depends on the extent to which one is connected to the word of God.

8. *The Law of Contagious Experience*

The law of contagious experience states that whenever the power of God is flowing and everyone is connected in the spirit, if one person catches the power or manifestations, the rest will catch it too. Do you know that if one person raises the dead in your church, other members and churches in the neighbourhood will catch it too such that within a twinkling of an eye, the whole city will be in a Holy Ghost flame. The manifestations of the spirit are contagious in the sense that they are easily transmitted to other people.

Some manifestations are common or popular amongst certain ministries as a result of the application of the law of contagious experience. There is a spiritual law in principle that we don't really know anything until we have experienced it. You can know something through somebody else's sharing or through reading the Word of God but we do not really know the matter until we have experienced it. God is a person and He wants us to experience Him as a person. For example, your relationship with your wife is a legal relationship but at the same time, it is a personal relationship. A house is a house but the relationships within the house make it a home. Christianity is a true-life relationship with God. When you experience God, you experience Him in the spiritual world, which has a side effect on our soul and on our body. Likewise, we can never really understand working with angels until we have had a spiritual contact and experience with them. However, we cannot base theology on experience. Theology must be based on the Word of God. But the experience helps us to look at the Word in a different way. Without the experience, I believe none of us will look at the Word in a different way.

Many people were former hard nut anti Charismatic. One day they became hungry for God. God touched them and they changed their view, which all the theology, arguments and persuasions in the world could not do so. It only takes one experience to change them. As a result, they re-aligned their whole thinking. One good example is the apostle Paul who was a great intellectual in his time. No amount of arguments or reasoning could have converted him. But one awesome experience with the Lord Jesus Christ on the way to Damascus was enough to change him. Paul did not base his theology on experience. However, his experience made him go back to re-study his theology. Our theology needs to be restudied from time to time. Sometimes our theology hinders us from the experiences of God, especially when it is a wrong theology. We do not base on theology or our experiences but we recognize that experiences help us and inspire us to look at the Word of God in ways we never look at before.

9. *The Law of Association*

It is an undeniable fact that the power of God flows through association or relationships hence Paul declared in 1 Corinthians 11:1 that *imitate me as I imitate Jesus*. Through this principle, power was able to flow from Paul to the churches. As they emulated him, they were thrust into the same degree of power at which he was operating. The Bible says, *"Now when they saw the boldness of Peter and John, and perceived that they were unlearned and ignorant men, they marvelled; and they took knowledge of them, that they <u>had been with Jesus</u>"* (Acts

4.13). In the context of this scripture, the phrase, *"had been with Jesus"* speaks of the *law of association*. In other words, it is because of their association with Jesus that people took heed of their message. Moreover, the Bible says *Joshua son of Nun was full of the spirit of wisdom; for Moses had laid his hands upon him: and the children of Israel hearkened unto him, and did as the LORD commanded Moses"* (Deuteronomy 34:9). This implies that it was because of his association with Moses that the people hearkened to the voice of Joshua. Every time they looked at Joshua, they saw Moses in him. This is just how powerful the law of contagious association is. Moreover, Elisha received the mantle by virtue of association with Elijah. If it wasn't for association, I don't believe he would have received even the *double portion* from him. He followed Elijah closely as he ate from his hand until the reward time came and Elisha scooped the spoils.

It is a divine truth that in order to move in greater dimensions of power, you need to be part of people or church that moves in power. Corporate anointing comes through the law of association. It is for this reason that Paul warned believers in Hebrews 10:25 *not to neglect the gathering of saints*. David further describes how pleasant it is for brethren to fellowship or associate together. As you enter into the season of the supernatural, God will cause your relationships to change because one key to becoming a carrier of God's power is not to be emotionally tied to people who are potential obstacles to your receiving and flowing in the power especially if those people have a traditional, denominational and rigid mentality that keeps them from changing for the better. By virtue of association, even the blessings of God can spill over to touch those close to you in your sphere of contact in the same way Lot got blessed by virtue of his association with Abraham and Laban got blessed because of Jacob (Genesis 30:25-43).

10. *The law of influence*

The power of God can flow mightily upon a person by virtue of putting oneself under a particular spiritual covering. Coming under a spiritual covering can cause one to flow in the same dimension of power as the pastor or leader of the church. In 1 Samuel 19:23, the Bible records a remarkable story about *Saul who was not a prophet but when he joined or came under the influence of prophets, he too started prophesying* until people were amazed. When he came under the spiritual covering of the prophets, he received a prophetic impartation and started prophesying. Through the *law of influence*, it is possible that if someone comes under the spiritual covering of a healer, he can operate in the gift of healing even if he is not a healer. It is through the law of influence that as God bless us, those who are our immediate sphere of influence or contact get to be blessed too. This is what we call *a spill over of blessings*. There is a realm in which you can get to determine everything that happens in your street and as you continue to dwell in the presence of God, your sphere of influence enlarges to the extent that you are able to influence the whole city. I read of how God used Smith Wigglesworth mightily to such an extent that he permitted no one in his locality to die without his permission. This is to show you how broad his sphere of influence had extended. Some people command authority over cities, others over regions, while others over continents. Your sphere of influence is determined by the degree of authority you can command in the realm of the spirit as well as the size of your God-given dream.

11. *The law of atmosphere*

A conducive atmosphere, ambiance and spiritual climate must be fostered in an endeavour to trigger the flow of God's power. God has always been known to speak from the cloud of His glory, hence it is important to know how to build a spiritual atmosphere. The spiritual atmosphere is the cloud of God's presence that surrounds us. We must therefore create a celestial atmosphere for miracles, signs and wonders through the word we speak. When you get to a level where your faith cannot operate, change the atmosphere. Unfortunately, many people are in places where the supernatural power is non-existent because a divine atmosphere was never generated. The atmosphere is generated through a myriad of spiritual exercises such as praise and worship, prayer and intercession which build the tabernacle where God's glory can manifest. After man was disconnected from the glory of God as a result of sin, the only way to bring it back was through praise and worship. However, the duration of praise and worship depends on the extent to which the environment or atmosphere is cultivated. If the atmosphere is hard to pierce, it will take longer to build the throne but where an atmosphere already exists, one can go directly into worship. Moreover, it is also important to discern the atmosphere whether it is for miracles, healing, deliverance or something else after that speak into that atmosphere in order to make what you declare come to pass. In Genesis 1:1-10, when God spoke and said *let there be light*, the Holy Spirit who had already created a conducive atmosphere by brooding over the face of the deep, acted on the word which God spoke and brought those things which God spoke into manifestation. This is the same principle by

Spiritual Laws & Principles of The Kingdom

which we operate in the realm of the miraculous whenever we want to provoke a greater flow of God's power.

12. *The law of confession*

The first law of operating in the power of God is to understand the power of words. Words are the capsules that contain the believer's anointing and release it forth. The believer's anointing in all realms of power depends on the word we speak. The next time you want to release the believer's anointing over anything, speak it out verbally. You know you are releasing tremendous authority and power over substances that you partake of. The law of confession is one of the most powerful ways in which you can be instantly catapulted into the realm of God's power. By definition, *"confession"* refers to the prophetic declaration, proclamation, pronunciation and utterance of God's word with a view to effecting changes in our situations and circumstances by the use of our tongue. In a practical sense, it means speaking forth the word of God from the depths of our spirits with the intent to change the prevailing situation and circumstances and to produce the results the word of God talks about. The word *"confession"* comes from the Greek word homologous, which means confessing the word of God. The word *homo* means same and *logos* means the word of God. *Homologous* therefore means confessing with the words of our mouth or saying exactly the same words that God says. The Bible declares in Proverbs 18:21 that death and life are in the power of the tongue. This means that confession is a powerful creative force, which can catapult a man to the highest realms and dimensions of power.

Therefore, since you can only receive what you confess in the realm of God's power, talking is very important because your words will reap a harvest. Philosophically speaking, your mouth rules in the realm of God's power, since the demonstration of power depends on what you say. Words were not made primarily for communication purposes; that is secondary. Instead, words were given specifically to release creative power in your spirit. In essence, words are God's method of operation by which He accomplishes His will, purpose and desire. There are pipelines for divine exploits. Words set spiritual laws in motion. Words are spiritual containers that carry power. Words are seeds sown with your mouth that produce their own kind. Words are the process starters of life. Words are the building blocks with which you construct your life and future. Words set the cornerstones of your life. Words program the human spirit for exploits. Words have creative ability. They create the realities you see. God's word—the incorruptible seed – has within it the ability and DNA to cause itself to come to pass. This means that God's word has potency to produce what it talks about. Just by speaking God's word alone is enough to turn around the situation. In Luke 7:6-7, the centurion pleaded with Jesus saying, *"I do not even think of myself worthy to come to you but say the word and my servant will be healed"*. Note that the centurion wasn't asking Jesus to say just anything; instead he was asking Him to speak God's word to turn around his situation. In today; language what the centurion was saying is, *"Lord, your word is just enough to change my situation"* and because He took God at His word, he was labelled as the one with the greatest faith in Israel simply because he believed in confessing God's word. Faith could therefore be best described as speaking God's word with intent to change situations and circumstances.

To cement this revelation with reference to scriptural evidence, Jesus declared in Mark 11:23, *"If you say to a mountain be thou removed and be cast into the sea and you do not doubt but believe that those things which you say shall come to pass, then you shall have whatever you say."* This implies that if you don't say it, then you cannot have it. If you can't confess that you are a miracle worker, then you cannot become one. If you do not confess power, you cannot have power. Words establish strongholds, break habits, change things and redirect thought patterns. Words point you in whatever direction they are aimed and released. Words set the course of your life. Words determine your future, your health, your wealth and your place in eternity. Words arrive at your future before you do. Words create desires and transmit images that you will eventually live out. Words frame your world. Words spoken today become a living reality tomorrow. Words give permission and licence to spiritual forces to work for you or against you. Words make demands on the blessing or the curse—whichever you call for. Words are goal setters that give direction and establish destination. Words are our method of operation, by which God accomplishes His will, purpose and desire for our lives. Words can turn around any situation. As a matter of fact, there is nothing on this earth so great or so powerful, including the physical body, which cannot be turned around by our words. Even death can be reversed by words; that is why the Bible says *death and life are in the power of the tongue.* The entire course of nature and the circumstances surrounding every human being are controlled by that person's words. We don't have a choice whether or not we live by words. We do, however, have a choice of what words we live by. If your mouth will feed your heart the word of faith when you don't need it—your heart will feed your mouth the word of faith when you do need it. We appropriate what is ours in Christ by making God's word a daily part of our vocabulary.

Spiritual Laws & Principles of The Kingdom

We are to confess what we can do in Christ, who we are in Christ and what we have in Christ.

13. The Law of desire

It must be understood that according to this spiritual law, spiritual things whether blessings, power or gifts are given by desire. Those who genuinely desire God's supernatural power are the best candidates for receiving it. In the natural realm if we feel hunger, we tend to forget the norms of courtesy because we seek only to satisfy our yearnings. The same happens in the spirit realm. Only those who hunger or thirst for the power are the candidates to receive it. You must have a desire, passion or an inspiration to become a miracle worker for, without the desire or passion, your dream to launch the world into an arena of divine exploits, won't have a long-lasting effect. As a matter of fact, the Bible says in Psalms 37:4 that *God will grant the desires of your heart* but if you don't have any desire to move in the supernatural realm, what do you expect God to work with? Therefore, your dream has to be watered by desire, which is like fire that ignites your spirit and keeps your dream ablaze. A perennial hunger, insatiable appetite and unquenchable thirst can manifest in any individual provided he is fully aware of his personal need to receive something. In 1 Samuel 1:5, *Elkanah's wife by the name of Hannah, was so desperately in need of a baby to the extent that it absorbed her consciousness* such that when she prayed, she looked as if she was drunk. This is the extent to which a desire can overwhelm a person. You see, there is a dimension that you can reach in the spirit whereby your desire to move in God's power and raise the dead gets so ingrained in your consciousness such that even your pastor will not understand you. Jacob desired the blessing to the extent of wrestling with an angel and breaking his hip because he desperately needed a blessing from God. Unless you are desperate for the power, anointing or the miraculous, you might not fully partake of it because the realm of the miraculous is provoked by desire. The extent to which you may receive from God is determined by how hungry or thirsty you are for the miraculous. It is therefore advisable that you develop an insatiable appetite for the supernatural in order to receive an avalanche of God's power.

14. The Law of preparation

The survival of the church depends on the degree of preparation it undertakes in order to walk in the supernatural. The truth is that in this end time season, God is raising a new generation of believers who knows how to walk in the dimension of eternity and know how to draw forth the wealth of the spiritual world. All men who walk in the supernatural realm, walk on their knees. The man of God on his knees sees further than a philosopher in her tiptoes. Behind the scenes, there is preparation time spent in hours of prayer, studying the word, meditation, praise and worship and so forth. It is during this time in God's presence that the Holy Spirit gives prophetic instruction on what He wants to do with His people, how He wants to do it and the direction in which He wants to take the church. Whether He wants to heal certain sickness, baptise people in the Holy Ghost, speak prophetic words or conduct deliverance, all these instructions are given at preparation stage. At times when people see a man of God moving in power, they think that power just rained down on him from Heaven and in the process they loose sight of the hours of preparation that are needed to before one could start ministering.

Even the coming of the Holy Ghost at Pentecost needed preparation because prior to His coming, the apostles had to spent hours of prayer in the upper room. Some people are eager to demonstrate the power of God but are not able to do so because they neither prepare nor spend time in the presence of God. It must be therefore understood that the power of God is not magic which just falls mysteriously from nowhere. Instead, it requires a significant level of preparation in order to provoke its flow. I experienced many encounters and many moments of God's power during my early years as a Christian. Those encounters shaped who I am today. God's timing is perfect and His preparations are essential. However, preparations don't earn the anointing; they simply enable us to carry it for the long haul.

15. *The Law of activation*

It must be understood that the power of Gods need to be provoked, activated and cultivated in order to flow or operate. Likewise, the spirit realm needs to be stirred, provoked in order to loose the power or blessings. This is the same principle by which *an angel of the lord had to come and stir the waters of the pool of Siloam* (John 5:4). Unless and if the waters of the pool were stirred up, he healing virtue would not manifest. By the same token, unless and if the power of God is stirred up in your spirit, it would not manifest. However, the pool was a shadow or portrait of the healing waters that would then flow from the Throne Room of Heaven upon the masses following the resurrection of the Lord Jesus Christ from the dead. The pool of Siloam is no longer a physical location. Instead, it is now in your spirit. Therefore, stir up the healing waters in your spirit and let them flow out as rivers to touch those in your sphere of contact. Do you remember that God declared through the voice of Prophet Hagai saying, *Once more and in a little while I will*

Spiritual Laws & Principles of The Kingdom

shake the Heavens, sea, earth and the desire of all nations shall come to me (Hagai 2:8). Do you notice that it is through shaking, stirring and activation that souls are ushered into the kingdom and that the power of God is manifested? In the absence of a shaking, souls would not come to the Kingdom. That is why it is important that we release a rumbling Heavenly sound piercing through the corridors of the realm spirit, dismantling the demonic thrones, so that souls will be released into the Kingdom.

It is scripturally evident that the power of God needs to be stirred up in order to flow. It is for this reason that Jude advised us to pray in the Holy Ghost because when you pray in other tongues, you energise or activate your spirit thereby allowing rivers of living waters to flow from within the depths of your spirit. This parallels Paul's declaration in Romans 8:11 that, *"If the same spirit that raised Jesus from the dead dwells in us, then He that raised Jesus from the dead shall also vitalise our mortal bodies"*. In its original context, the word, *"vitalise"* means to activate, to stir up or quicken. Hence, it is the nature of the indwelling presence of the Holy Spirit to activate, stir up and invigorate those who are spirit filled so that they can move in the direction of the Spirit. In a ministerial context, there are people who are called and gifted by God in the fivefold ministry but they may never be able to move and operate in the dimension of those gifts until they are activated and stirred up. That is why it is important to activate the gifts of the spirit in people's lives because some gifts are just dormant, idle and underutilised. The same applies to some blessings which are situated in the realm of the spirit. Such blessings need to be stirred up in order to rain upon people's lives. This is the reason behind revivals because every revival is meant to stir up or loose God's blessings that have remained dormant, untapped or intercepted in the spirit realm.

16. *The Law of Manifestation and experimentation*

It is a spiritual principle that miracles must be declared the minute they manifest. Major manifestations of God's supernatural power are evident today but only those that are declared and confirmed will have a long lasting effect in the realm of the spirit. The greatest challenge that is limiting people from walking in the realm of the miraculous is that miracles are happening but they are never declared. Some people receive miracles and never testify about them. This causes them to lose them a short time later because if a miracle is not declared, its presence in the natural realm becomes illegal.

Apostle Frequency Revelator

The truth is that the power of God flows through manifestations. A manifestation is a sign of the flow of God's power. Jesus said in Mark 16:17-18 that *these signs will manifest to them whom believe, in My Name, they will cast out devils, speak in new tongues and when they eat anything deadly, it shall by no means hurt them.* This implies that whenever the power of God is displayed, there are signs or manifestations that authenticate the flow of that power. The power of God cannot be hidden in the same way a city on a hill cannot be hidden. Jesus said in Luke 8:16 that, *no one lights a candle and put it under the table.* This is because light is originally designed to manifest and now that you are the light of the world, your light, which speaks of your influence should extend beyond borders. Do you know that when Moses said to God, *"Lord show me your Glory"* in Exodus 33:18-23, he actually challenged God on the basis of the law of manifestation? In other words, he was challenging God to manifest His power. This is to tell you that the power of God should be manifested all the times for the glory of God to be revealed amongst mankind.

Another dimension of manifestation is what I call *experimentation*. It is an undeniable fact that the power of God flows through experimentation. It must be understood that the power, anointing or blessings exist as realities in the spirit realm but the means to cause them to manifest in the natural realm is through experimentation. Demonstration of actions of faith is what releases the spirit realm. In Matthew 10:8, Jesus gave an instruction that, *"Go heal the sick, raise the dead, cast out devils. Freely you have received and freely you shall give".* The word *give"* in this context speaks of demonstration of power because it was said when Jesus was talking about moving in signs and wonders. In other words, what Jesus meant was that as you have received the power freely, you must also freely demonstrate it. As the power of God is demonstrated, more taps of power are opened and flows into our lives. If you receive the power of God and you do nothing about it, you will not be able to receive more. But as you release it, more power comes. Do you remember that God said *test Me and see if I'm not able.* This tells me that the power of God's blessings is triggered by testing or experimentation. Note that this does not apply to the release of financial blessings only but to the release of God's power as well. Unless and if you test Him, you may never know the power of the blessing which He can release upon your life.

It must be understood in this regard that the word of God is not a historical database of stories. Instead, it is a collection of revelation and divine insights from the word of God. Therefore, to prove that the word of God is alive, we must demonstrate or experiment it. Demonstration means making the word practical to produce the results of what it talks about. However, the greatest challenge that we have in the body of Christ is that preachers are teaching theoretical concepts of the word but they never get to a point where they practically demonstrate it, to prove that what they are preaching is really from God. The word of God was never meant to be a theoretical concept but a practical phenomenon. Therefore, don't just preach the word but prove its validity and authenticity by demonstrating its power as Paul ascertained.

17. *Law of faith*

Faith is such a tremendous force that can pull down the blessings and power of God from the realm of the spirit into the natural realm. The word declares in Ephesians 1:3 that *we are blessed with all spiritual blessings in heavenly places*. But how we get them to manifest from the spirit realm into the physical is by the *law of faith*. Faith transcends both realms of existence. It is a force or invisible hand that moves in the realm of the spirit to harness God's power and then brings it to manifestation in the natural world. Without faith it is impossible to please God. In a similar vein, without faith, it is impossible to move in power because anything done outside the context of faith is dead. When you bring all the fullness of hope into actualising, it is the law of faith working and it brings you into the first realm, the outer court. As you begin to go faithfully into that realm, faith becomes second nature to you. Then you enter into the second realm, faith naturalised. It becomes so natural in you that you live above the law because you fulfil the law and you enter into the divine presence of His love. It is a spiritual principle that miracles exist in the now. Sadly, some preachers preach miracles in the future and speak them in a future tense saying God will heal you, God will visit us, hence by so doing they have caused miracles to be delayed. Rarely do they declare what God is doing and saying now. This is not how faith should operate. Therefore, if you want to see a greater manifestation of miracles in your life, church or ministry, simply believe God for the impossible and you will force the hand of God to move on your behalf.

It is a typical scenario that so many believers get so obsessed about confession such that they just confess and confess and yet ignore the crucial element that is responsible to make their confession work, which is *faith*. If you have confessed the word of God but you do not see any results of your confession, then know that there is a second factor that controls it. Don't forget the first part that says, *"Those who believe in My name,"* that is, your faith level. Your faith level controls the amount of believer's anointing released when you speak His word. If your faith level is small even though your words are big and loud but a lot of doubts behind your mind and in your heart, the anointing released is just a trickle. It is not the loudness of your words that determines the power content. Sometimes when you take authority, you can't help it if your voice does get higher or louder. But it is not just the loudness of the voice the demon obeys. But if you don't have faith, you tend to copy the method but not the principles, hence you are heading for disaster. If you want to copy, then copy the principles. And then if you don't have other methods go ahead and copy them but develop your own method

As aforementioned, it's not just the loudness of the voice of the minister although when you exercise authority you do tend to get louder. But it's the faith level behind the spoken words that get the job done. Now, notice how the believer's authority operates in Mark 11:23 *For assuredly, I say to you, whoever says to this mountain, "Be removed and be cast into the sea and does not doubt in his heart, but believes that those things he says will be done, he will have whatever he says.*

Let me take the middle part and expand on it because that is the part that is not very clear to many people. It says, "*....but believes that those things he says will be done*". Let me pull that whole phrase out because it has to be seen clearly. It says, "*...believes that those things he says will come to pass.*" It's different from believing that what he believes will come to pass. It did not say, "*but believes that what he believes come to pass.*" That's what a lot of people are doing. They think they are in Mark 11:22-24 but they actually are acting on Mark chapter zero verse zero, neither here nor there. Mark 11:23 says, "*But believes that those thing he says will come to pass*". Instead, a lot of believers are believing that what they believe will come to pass. They are exercising faith on something inside instead of something they released.

You may do that when you are operating in the anointing upon because the anointing upon is a different realm. But the believer's anointing will not permit you to do that. You must believe that what you say is already coming to pass. And the better way of releasing it is this: You will come to a sick person, even if that person doesn't show any symptom of recovery, and say, "*In Jesus' name be healed,*" and exercise all your faith in the words you say going through the person. You cannot be exercising much faith in your own words if you doubt your own words. You have to keep repeating them to encourage your own faith. They can believe that what they believe will one day come to pass. But they find it difficult to believe in the words that they say. So, the words that they say they have to exercise a little bit of faith. They have some faith in God and some faith in their heart but they have no faith in their own words.

To cement this divine revelation with reference to further scriptural evidence, lets refer to Mark 11:23, *Whoever says if you have faith as a mustard seed you will say to this mountain be removed and be cast into the sea and if he does not believe in his heart but believe in his own words it will come to pass.* Do you notice that what provokes God's power to move the mountain is believing in your own words? Do you know people don't believe in their own words? That's the problem. If you don't believe your own words, then you cancel your own anointing. When you release the believer's anointing, the faith level is determined. So, the next time you prepare yourself and if you are casting out a demon, you get more results if you treat your words like bullets. If you don't value your own words in the same way a soldier value bullets, you will have no effect. Treat your words like bullets that are thrown out. The next time you release a believer's anointing, treat your words like bullets. A lot of believers' tongues are too loose. In fact, their tongues are so loose that they are dragging the ground. Their words have lost its power. Your words are like bullets. If you use them carefully they are going to be powerful. So, when you pray to cast out demons, heal the sick or raise the dead, believe in your own words. You come and you say, *In Jesus' name, come out,*" whether you scream or shout or say softly, the demon may do whatever he wants but you just walk off. And if you walk off believing in the power of your own words that fellow will recover. We will need to waste less time trying to work ourselves up.

18. *The law of focusing*

The Bible records an incident in Exodus 3: 2 whereby the angel of the Lord appeared to Moses in a flame of fire in the bush and instantly, He turned aside from what he was doing to see this bush burning. Acknowledging the angel's presence involves giving him your full attention. Turning aside from whatever that is taking your attention and giving it your full attention. This is the essence of the spiritual *law of focusing*. Moses saw the bush burning for a long time but it's only when he came near the bush that he said, *"I must see why the bush is burning and yet it is not consumed."* See, he didn't know it was God yet. All he saw was a spectacular phenomenon. When he zoomed in on the phenomena, he received the details. And as he came near the bush, he heard the bush say, *"Moses, Moses,"* and that encounter marked the beginning of God's call for his life. You see, we have to zoom in before we get other details. When you look at something, it becomes more detailed. It's just like you could be passing a lot of scenery and you are not really paying any attention. But then when you focus on this **specific** plant and you began to see its condition, you begin to pay attention. It is the principle of *focusing*.

The truth is that when you don't put aside those things and focus on what God is bringing to your attention, you may loose it. Figuratively speaking, sometimes it's just a telephone ringing. There is no message yet, but the telephone is ringing. You got to pick it up. You got to pay attention and focus. Picking it up is like paying attention to those things. Sometimes in the spirit world you could be praying. And as you are praying, your attention is drawn towards something. Your mind and your will have a free choice. You could choose not to be drawn towards that. The bush could be burning and you could choose not to be drawn towards that, hence you may loose it. He wants you to turn aside and focus you attention on that something He has drawn you to. There is something that catches your attention first and you need to focus on this thing. You acknowledge by turning aside and paying attention to whatever is catching your mind. God gives you a free choice. If you respond then He would also respond.

The question that you are probably asking yourself is: How did Moses respond? As he drew near to the burning bush, the Lord called out from the burning bush, *"Moses, Moses."*. Moses could have responded in different ways to that call. One of the possible responses is to run. To some of you as you walk by a tree and the tree calls you, you may wonder, *"Who was that?"*
You may respond differently or rush to collect a horse pipe in order to try and extinguish the burning flame. You could run away or you could find out what that voice is and what the spectacular burning bush is all about. Somehow Moses responded wisely and said, *"Here I am."* He doesn't even know who is there. But whoever that was knew him. If you happen to pass by a bush and someone calls you by name, some may think it's the devil hiding behind the bush trying to trap you. If you are in a supermarket and some stranger calls you, you don't challenge them, you respond, yet because they are invisible we don't respond the same way.

Law of timing

As stipulated by His times and seasons, God does not do the same thing all the time. In order for us to be recipients of a torrential flow of His power, we therefore need to be sensitive to what He is doing at a particular time. Concerning the timing of the release of God's power on earth, God spoke through the Prophet Zechariah saying, *"Ask for me in the time*

Spiritual Laws & Principles of The Kingdom

of the latter rain and I will give you showers of rain." In the context of this scripture, rain speaks of God's power or anointing. The fact that God says we should ask for rain *during the time of rain* means it's not every time that it rains. God operates in times and seasons; hence if you ask for rain at such a time when it's not the season of rain, you will not receive a positive response. It matters most when you ask for rain at the right time and God promises that when the correct timing is adhered to as per His calendar; the rain of power will come.

The law of timing implies doing the right thing at the right time. However, the truth is that at times people are doing the right thing but at the wrong time. A wrong timing might either result in a delay or procrastination of a blessing or a total failure for a blessing to be dispatched. The reason why many believers have not been able to receive their blessings despite the fact that they prayed and fasted is because of a lack of understanding of the law of timing. Unlike the sons of Issachar who had an acute understanding of times and seasons, hence knew what Israel ought to do at a particular time, many people do not understand or know God's timing yet it is such a critical determinant in matters of moving in God's power. Timing is very important when it comes to matters of the miraculous because just like the sons of Issachar, you need an acute understanding of what to do, how to do it and when to do it. For example, you need to understand how to channel the power of God in the direction of the Spirit. Wrong timing might yield wrong results.

In a ministerial context, there is a time during a meeting whereby you can sense that the *cloud* has been fully saturated. It is probably the best time to release God's power or anointing upon the congregants. Sadly, many do not experience the spectacular display of power because they are too quick to demonstrate the power of God when the river of God's anointing is not even flowing. On the extreme end of scale, there are those who get too stuck in their own church programmes and agendas such that by the time they finish and want to move in power, the wave of glory would have sailed by, leaving only a residue of God's presence. This is to tell you that you need to be sensitive when you are ministering so that you don't just demonstrate the power of God anyhow, but wait for that moment when the atmosphere is Heavenly pregnant with the glory of God. It is at that time that you can know that even angels are ready to release the glory of God in abundance, hence you may not waste any time but release the contents of Heaven right on the scene.

19. Law of action and reaction

The law of action and reaction brings to light the fact that what we do in the spirit realm will always elicit a corresponding response in the natural and whatever we do in the natural is always preceded by a corresponding action in the Spirit. Did you know that God works by what you give Him? Likewise, angles work according to the word that you speak and if you don't say anything, they cannot produce anything for you in the spirit realm because they need your input to generate output. The greater truth is that Heaven responds by what the earth sends forth. In the natural realm, rain can only come when enough humidity has been released into the atmosphere to generate clouds. By the same token, if you need to receive anything from God or Heaven, including power, you must send something as an input in the form of prayers, fasting, consecration and meditation and other spiritual exercises that provokes a divine exchange of God's power. This is how a revival breaks out, to bring the earth to a perfect alignment with the Heavenly realm. When the earth is no longer working in perfect synchronisation with Heavens, it is a sign that a rival is needed. Jesus made it explicitly clear in Mathew 18:18, that *whatever we bind on earth shall be bound in heaven and whatever we loose on earth shall be loosed in heaven.* This is the basis of the principle of action and reaction. In other words, as you take a step of faith to release power in the natural realm, there is a corresponding action that authenticates your loosing from the Heavenly realm.

Action and reaction states that for every action you take in the supernatural realm, there will always be a corresponding reaction to that action in the natural realm. The Bible proclaims in Luke 6:38: *Give, and it shall be given unto you; good measure, pressed down, and shaken together, and running over, shall men give unto your bosom.* It further says: *ask and it shall be given to you, knock and the door shall be opened.* This implies that there is a response in the spirit realm to every action of faith that you take in the natural realm. Giving is a spiritual act and, as you act on it, there is a corresponding response that you receive in the natural realm in the form of blessings. That is why what we do in the realm of the spirit will always elicit a corresponding response in the natural and whatever we do in the natural is always preceded by a corresponding action in the Spirit. The law of action and reaction brings the realm of the natural and realm of the Spirit to work together. Revivals are triggered in this way. Do you know that people always react

Spiritual Laws & Principles of The Kingdom

differently when the power of God is manifested? Consider how people reacted when the lightning of God's power was manifested on the way to Damascus in Acts. Some said it thundered, others said it roared and others just did not have a clue as to what exactly transpired. This reinforces the fact that for every action in the supernatural realm, there is always a corresponding reaction in the natural realm although it might be manifested differently.

Another dimension to this divine principle is the law of *yielding*. In the spirit world, whatever you try hard to do or to get using your own effort might never materialise. The spirit world works more by yielding than by trying. Every time you try too hard, you might find it hard to infiltrate the realms of the spirit. It is for this reason that God spoke to Zerrubabel saying, *"it's not by might nor by power but by My spirit"*. In the spirit world, God's power manifested through the anointing is more achieved by yielding and receiving rather than trying and grabbing. There are times when the Holy Spirit is addressing deep-seated emotional issues in the meeting even without a manifestation. If it's not God's will for us to have a specific manifestation that we are all looking for on a given day, then let's not twist God's hand.

Even the angelic realm does not work by trying and snatching, whiffing and huffing. Instead, it works by yielding to the ministry of angels. It must therefore be clear that we do not try to see angels. We don't even force an angelic appearance at all. Instead, just be aware of how to work with angels and be sensitive to their presence and as you grow in that knowledge and in the things of God, you will get to a level where you see angels and interact with them in the same way you engage your friends.

20. *The law of relationship.*

It is worth exploring the divine truth that everything in the spirit realm flows from a place of relationship. Prayer is a place of relationship. Giving flows though relationship. Power, anointing, glory and any other spiritual substance flows through a relationship with God. Relationship is what determines the nature, capacity and magnitude of blessings and power we can receive from God. Promotion and divine elevation comes through deepening a relationship with the father. The deeper the relationship, the greater the power. All spiritual blessings come through relationship called a covenant. There are certain things which a man can never receive from God as long as he does not have a relationship with Him. Worship comes though relationship with the father. Without relationship there is no Christianity. In essence Christianity is not a religion as people presume but a relationship based on power. This is the reason why above all else Jesus emphasized more on the relations with the father. Jesus proclaimed that everything that He does is a result of a relationship He has with the father. Even in the present time, ministries are built through relationships, blessings come through relationships, visions are shared through relationships, and impartation comes through relationship. In the spirit realm, one is known by virtue of His degree of relationship with Jesus. This is the reason why the demon said to the sons of Sceva, *"Jesus I know Paul I know but who are you?",* because they did not have a relationship with Jesus. Hence, they ended up suffering the consequences. The church needs to come to a place where they treasure, value and take advantage of relationships more that never before. Therefore, if you want to plunge into greater depths of the miraculous, you need to understand the power of relationship and harness that power to invade deeper territories in the supernatural.

CHAPTER TWO

SPIRITUAL LAWS AND PRINCIPLES OF PROSPERITY

Divine Principles For Manifesting Millions In The Natural Realm

This section presents a revelation of key spiritual laws and principles of Kingdom prosperity, which one could apply with a view to living a life of superabundance, progress, success, increase, promotion, advancement and enrichment in every sphere of human endeavour. It is, therefore, an acute understanding of these spiritual laws and principles that will determine the amount of blessing you can receive from God and that will ultimately catapult you to a position where you can amass a wealth of financial resources to become a Kingdom millionaire in your generation.

Many people across a broad spectrum of the Christian faith desire to be millionaires but they do not become millionaires because of their failure to understand God's spiritual laws and principles of prosperity, which they could apply or take advantage of to tap into the realm of millionaires. For example, it is a typical scenario in charismatic Christian circles that some Christians cry, fast and pray for a financial breakthrough but their financial status never changes because they don't know how to apply the spiritual laws of wealth making. The truth of the matter is that there are certain spiritual laws you must practically apply or follow to make wealth. If you don't apply them, you can never be millionaire. In the same way that a farmer plants a seed in the ground and a plant will spring up for him based on the principles of seedtime and harvest time, anybody can become a millionaire provided he correctly applies the principles of prosperity. Unfortunately, some unbelievers become more financially successful than believers because they have learnt the proper principles of prosperity to follow. The failure of some believers to follow the correct principles of prosperity could be attributable to misconstrued traditional teachings in some Christian charismatic circles, where some believers have been incorrectly taught that every blessing comes through fasting and prayer. While to a certain extent this could appeal to matters of faith in terms of enhancing spiritual sensitivity and tuning one's spirit to receive spiritual blessings, the greater truth is that there is a time and place for fasting and prayer but the actual manifestation of wealth comes as a result of the proper and meticulous application of spiritual laws.

It must therefore be expressly understood that having a dream to become a millionaire is one thing but the actual process of implementing the spiritual laws of prosperity is a different task all together. On that note, it is highly advisable that one should not just have a desire or dream but should go beyond that level to acquire revelation knowledge of which spiritual laws and principles to apply, how they should be applied and under what circumstances they should be applied. The good news is that God's spiritual laws have been tried, tested and proven and, when correctly applied, they are guaranteed to work in all circumstances regardless of who applies them. In essence, these principles are not just a theory or theological facts but time-tested, tried and true, and have really proven themselves.

It is of paramount importance to highlight from the outset that to generate alarming results of financial prosperity and abundance, you need to practise or exercise not just one of these laws but all of them. For example, the law of giving works hand in hand with the law of faith and righteousness. This means that if you can take authority over your giving, then you can also take authority over your receiving because all of these things—the right motive, faith, and sowing seed —work together. In other words, it's not just your right motive that will cause money and divine prosperity to be loosened to you. And it's not just faith, either. You could speak the word in faith all you want, but if there are no works, such as giving, behind your faith, your faith will be unproductive. Then there are those who give and give, but they don't know what belongs to them in Christ. They haven't received the revelation that prosperity is their right; therefore, they don't stand their ground in faith about it and prosperity often passes them by. In your quest to amass huge wealth from Heaven, you must, therefore, understand that all of these spiritual laws and principles work together to produce great wealth in your life.

21. *The law of planting and harvesting/sowing and reaping/giving and receiving*

This is an official legal principle by which blessings are received or released in the Kingdom of God. The law of reaping and sowing forms the basis of all spiritual transactions and divine exchanges that may take place between Heaven and earth. It is a supreme spiritual law that legalises or authenticates the validity of any spiritual transactions and exchanges involved in the distribution of wealth, financial resources and blessings between Heaven and other planets. Jesus said to a young man in Matthew 19:21, *"Go and sell that thou hast, and give to the poor, and thou shall have treasure in heaven."* This implies that you make a deposit into the heavenly account by sowing seed and then release your faith to make a withdrawal from the same heavenly bank account whenever you want it (Philippians 4:17-20; Matthew 6:19-21). There are many supernatural streams of provision and income available in God's Kingdom and giving is one supernatural act designed for us to reap supernatural things. It is a principle in the Kingdom that you receive to give and you give to receive, and this is the principal law that governs the system of operation of Heaven. This is the essence of the law of seedtime and harvest (Genesis 8:22; Mark 4:26-32). This is a law by which we can access Heaven's resources and abundance of wealth. In essence, it is a ticket that gives us legal claim and access to the wealth of Heaven.

The reason some people are not receiving from God is because they are not giving and the reason they are not giving is because they are not receiving and the reason they are not receiving is because they are not asking. This is a complex chain of action. The main reason for giving is receiving; hence, God demands that you must not give if you don't expect anything in return. Some give grudgingly, in disobedience, in wavering faith and without expecting anything specific in return; hence, they don't see the results of their giving. This is why at times some unbelievers have acquired resources that believers don't have because they have learnt to tap into the system of God's provision by correctly applying His spiritual laws and principles of prosperity. In view of the above, believers must therefore be awakened to a reality that spiritual laws and principles of God's prosperity or system of provision apply to the whole universe whether one is a believer or not. God honours above all else his word and will therefore grant anyone who puts it into practice the right to partake in His wealth regardless of that person's spiritual status or position. It is a greater truth that praying and fasting does not produce money or wealth; instead, it is a spiritual exercise designed specifically to sharpen or align your spirit to enable you to move efficiently in the realm of the Spirit to receive God's blessings.

The truth of the matter is that all things held constant, money is produced on the basis of the principle of giving and receiving. You give money to receive money and you receive money to give money. That's why even in worship God commanded people not to come to His house empty-handed because He wants them to take advantage of this principle, which He has made freely available in the universe. In Leviticus 17:24, God went to the extent of commanding believers not to give a faulty sacrifice. This implies that there is an introspection and examination that is involved before giving offerings but this time it is not in the form of examining animals for defects as was the case in the olden days but examining ourselves without any ulterior motives or imperfection or grumbling. Contrary to what the majority of believers have been taught, giving should not be restricted to monetary offerings only but should include any substance of value that is deemed acceptable in the Kingdom. Therefore, if you aspire to be a Kingdom millionaire, then start giving whatever you have and God will give it back to you multiplied by millions. This is how millionaires are produced in the Kingdom.

It is evident from the above scriptures that giving is at the very heart of prosperity because a giving person is a prosperous person. Giving is the only spiritual practice that renders a supernatural escape or bail out from the calamities of life manifested through lack, poverty and debt. This is why Paul declared in 2 Corinthians 9:11 (as written in the NIV Bible) that *[As a result of your giving] you will be enriched in every way so that you can be generous on every occasion, and through us your generosity will result in thanksgiving to God.* Moreover, giving is the only area in the Bible where God opens His doors wide for humanity to challenge Him, test Him or try Him. He declared in Malachi 3:10-12: *"Test me and see if I will not open you the windows of heaven, the torrents of heaven, and pour you out a blessing after blessing, eve unto abundance, that there shall not be room enough to receive or store it."* It must be understood in the context of this scripture that the tithe is something you owe but the offering is a seed you sow. The King-

Spiritual Laws & Principles of The Kingdom

dom of Heaven operates on the principle of sowing and reaping. If you are a giving person, God will put it in people's hearts to bless you with anything that you need. Why? Because of your seed in the ground—because you've continually sown seeds by your giving. If you take authority over your giving, God will take authority over your receiving for you. Therefore, if you aspire to be a millionaire then make it a habit to give either to the poor or to the work of ministry and you will provoke God's supernatural financial provision in your life as God will repay you multiplied a million fold.

Some spiritual things work in conjunction with natural things, such as seedtime and harvest—the planting or sowing of seed and the reaping of a harvest. But then, some spiritual things work just the opposite of the natural way or the world's way. For example, the world's system is set up to get your hands on what you want whenever you can and hoard it. The world can't comprehend the notion of giving something away to get something. No, people have to take something and then hold on to it to have something. This is the economic principle of investment, which the world lives by. A person who lives by this principle can't understand the attitude that says, "Lord, make me a blessing, as a means of increasing." This person would rather say, "Lord, give me something. That's the only way I'm going to increase." God's spiritual laws often work opposite to the laws of the world's system. The world will lie, cheat, steal, withhold, and do everything it can to get ahead. But God tells us to give it up. This is because you can never be less than what you give, for the more you give, the more you receive. The Lord Jesus alluded to this when he said, *"Give and it shall be given unto you; good measure, pressed down, and shaken together, and running over, shall men give into your bosom. For with the same measure that ye mete withal it shall be measured to you again"* (Luke 6:38). Note that it doesn't say, *"...Shall GOD give into your bosom"*, but it says, *"...Shall MAN give into your bosom"*. This implies that it is your giving that moves the hand of God to touch the hearts of men to give back to you in abundance. The Bible further records in 1 Kings 3:4-5 that Solomon offered a thousand burnt offerings to God and this moved the Lord to visit him that same night and say to him, *"Ask what I should give you"*. In other words, he got a fat cheque from the Lord because of what he had given.

It is evident that the Kingdom of Heaven operates on the principle of sowing and reaping. The Bible declares that,

> *He which soweth sparingly shall reap also sparingly; and he which soweth bountifully shall reap also bountifully (2 Corinthians 9:6).*

In the context of this scripture, the word *"sparingly"* means a minimum, not much. Therefore, don't stay in the sparing harvest, instead, raise yourself to the level of your seed. That means in order to receive increase, give God more to work with. If you give Him a little, that's all He has to work with. You must therefore release a greater seed in order to release a greater harvest. This implies that you can't be ready for a harvest without having sown first. And you can't be ready for a big harvest without having sown big first. Contrary to what many people presume, giving is not about God but about you; it is meant to help you, not God, because some people think that they are doing God a favour by their giving, whereas in actual fact it is they who benefit from it, not God. Every time you use your money on God's behalf, it gives God the opportunity to give you more money. Some people wait to get more money so that they can start giving, and this is wrong. The best way to escape or get out of poverty and lack is to give, even when you have little. As a matter of fact, people who are bound in poverty are the ones who should give more and give their way out of poverty. The Bible describes in 2 Corinthians 8:2 *how that in a great trial of affliction the abundance of their joy and their deep poverty abounded [increased greatly] unto the riches of their liberality.* Paul was talking about money in this passage. He was actually talking about a giving grace. In the context of the above scripture, it is their liberality that brought them out of poverty. In other words, they were liberal in their giving even though they didn't have a whole lot to give and this is what triggered or provoked an avalanche of God's blessings on their lives. Some people want to wait until they have more money to give. But you have to start where you are today. You must have the giving grace first before you can have the receiving grace. There are no shortcuts. You can't receive first and then give. It doesn't work that way. It is the grace of giving that activates the grace of receiving. Your giving in faith moves the hand of God in your finances. Your responsibility is to obey; His responsibility is to bring it back to you.

23. *The law of multiplication and magnification*

This is a spiritual principle by which our blessings are multiplied, magnified, doubled and tripled in measures that are beyond what we have sown or given. In the realm of God's prosperity, the value of your giving is measured not by how much you have given but by the percentage of the total wealth that you have; hence, you don't necessarily have to receive in return the same amount that you have given, as is the case in the natural realm. Instead, you reciprocally receive a measure of blessing that has been magnified or multiplied beyond what you have given and just the little that you have sown can produce millions in wealth. The Bible says in 2 Corinthians 9:11 that,

> *He who supplies the seed to the sower and bread for food, shall supply and multiply the seed you have sown and increase the fruit of your righteousness.*

This is what we call, in the realm of prosperity, *the law of multiplication*. From a spiritual point of view, you need to understand how spiritual laws and principles are different from natural laws. In the realm of God's prosperity, when you give something, you don't necessarily have to give a million rand to receive millions. This is why in the realm of God's prosperity we become millionaires in the twinkling of an eye because our blessings are multiplied beyond natural measures or limitations. The Bible says in Genesis 26:12 that *Isaac sowed during the time of drought and in the same year he reaped a hundred fold*, meaning that whatever he sowed in small amounts, under unfavourably arid or dry conditions, was multiplied a hundred times. In other words, he received a hundred fold supernatural release. This spiritual law operates in conjunction with the law of favour to produce a supernatural torrent or downpour of God's blessings.

In the realm of God's prosperity, God gives you a measure beyond what you have invested. This is why He declared in Luke 6:38 that *a good measure pressed down shaken together will be poured back onto your lap*. This is the secret of success in the Kingdom, which many believers have not yet comprehended. Many people are reluctant to give and, hence, they have not been able to walk in the fullness of God's blessings because their minds are still focused on the natural law, which states that you can receive only what you have given. This is because they have not been able to grasp or catch a glimpse of the revelation of the law of multiplication, by which the seed that we sow is amplified, magnified and multiplied beyond natural measures. As a matter of fact, you must never give if you don't have an expectation that your giving will come back *multiplied a hundred fold* because giving was never designed for fun or for showing off; rather, the principal reason behind giving is multiplication. Moreover, you must give the exact amount that God has told you to give because if you give in disobedience, regardless of the size of your giving, it is not counted for anything in the Spirit.

To highlight some of the important features of the law of multiplication, God says in Psalms 68:35 that *one shall chase a thousand and two shall put ten thousand to flight.* And concerning our victory over enemies, God's word also says in Psalms 91:7 that *a thousand shall fall on my left hand and ten thousand on my right but no harm shall come near me.* This is the law of magnification and it works in both positive and negative situations. It must, therefore, be understood that God's mathematics is different from natural mathematics. In the realm of the natural, if one person chases a thousand people, it is logical that two will chase two thousand people, but according to God, if one chases a thousand, two will put ten thousand to flight. And if a thousand of people fall on my left, logic and natural mathematics tell you that another thousand will fall on my right hand for the scale or equation to balance, but, in the realm of God's prosperity, it is a completely different case altogether. This is to show you that you can achieve immensurable proportions of blessings in God by giving a little.

It is *God's nature to exceed your expectation* in every sphere of spiritual endeavour. That is why He says in Ephesians 3:20, "*I will do exceedingly and abundantly beyond what you ask, think or imagine.*" Why? Because His law of multiplication magnifies what you have given to immeasurable proportions. In Genesis 22:17 and Hebrews 6:14, God said to Abraham, "*Surely in blessings I will bless you and in multiplying I will multiply you.*" In a practical sense, this implies that you can pray for a job but God will give you a company; you pray for rent money but God gives you a house; you pray for a friend but God gives you a wife; you pray for an idea but He gives you a business; and you pray for thousands but He gives you millions; glory to God. Therefore, if you aspire to become a Kingdom Millionaire, then rightly position yourself in this season with an expectation that whatever you have given shall be multiplied and, as you command the hundredfold release over your giving, your wealth will be multiplied a million fold into an avalanche of riches and money in the best currencies of the world, back into your account.

24. *The law of the covenant of prosperity*

It must be understood that the basis of godly prosperity, provision, abundance and increase is the *law of the covenant.* It is a lack of understanding of God's grace and the covenant of His ever-present mercy that robs many people of the blessings of God. It is a spiritual fact that the blessings of the covenant are largely untapped by Christians today. It is a typical scenario in the body of Christ today that many people are tapping into other minor or trivial areas of blessings and in the process neglecting key financial blessings that come through the covenant. The Bible says in Galatians 3:13 that,

> *Christ has redeemed us by His blood and was made poor so that through his poverty, all the blessings of Abraham may come upon us.*

We are a seed of Abraham and all the blessings of Abraham are legitimately and rightfully ours, but there are certain blessings that a man can never receive from God unless he enters into a covenant with Him. These are the blessings of the covenant. In essence, there is a realm of God's blessings called the *covenant of blessings*. If you cross the border into this realm, you are ushered right into the arena of God's neverending provision and you function in the realm of superabundance. The moment you cross this boundary line, you provoke an unprecedented flow of blessings and thus tap into boundless opportunities and receive a special grace of prosperity to tap into every opportunity God provides.

This is a dimension in the realm of God where God begins to take you seriously. The minute a man enters into a covenant with God, all Heaven's attention and resources are directed towards him. When you move across the boundary line of God's blessings you don't work hard but reap a thousand fold with little effort just like *Isaac sowed during the time of drought and in the same year he reaped hundred fold* (Genesis 26:12). Entering into a covenant of God's blessings is equivalent to moving from the outer court to the inner court. In Genesis 12, God called Abraham out of His country and walked with him (Genesis 1 – 12) with nothing much happening. However, the minute he entered into a covenant with God (Genesis 15), God declared him the father of all nations.

If you are outside the boundary line of prosperity, you can work your fingers to the bone but you will hardly have any success. Through the law of the covenant of prosperity, we are partakers in the blessings of Abraham. The blessings in Abraham's life were a result of a covenant. The Bible says in Genesis 13:1 that Abraham was very rich in livestock and in silver and gold. This is because he made a covenant with God and because of the covenant even when Abraham made mistakes, silver and gold and livestock were poured abundantly on him because he was in a covenant with God. In

Genesis 26:12-13, it says that Isaac sowed in the land and reaped a hundred fold in the same year and the Lord blessed him. Why? Because of the covenant. If you take away the law of the covenant, all you have left is the law of sowing and reaping, which will not multiply that fast. After Isaac, Jacob also prospered because of the covenant. If it wasn't for the covenant, he would not have achieved the measure of success he did.

The law of the covenant is beyond the law of reaping and sowing, tithing and giving. You have to keep the law of tithing and giving together with the law of the covenant. It is not only keeping the law of sowing and reaping that matters but learning to move or migrate into a covenant and then keeping these spiritual laws. The covenant must, however, be invoked or activated in order to work for you. The Bible says in Exodus 2:24 that the Israelites came out of Egypt with prosperity, a lot of the silver and gold of Egypt, and the basis of all this prosperity was the covenant because the Bible says in Exodus 2:24 that God heard their groaning and He remembered his covenant. The Israelites were already working hard as slaves but what was causing them not to prosper was that their covenant was not activated or invoked. By the same token, there are Christians who work very hard but they don't seem to make ends meet because they don't know the covenant of prosperity. A covenant must be remembered and invoked. The Israelites remembered the formula and the principles but forgot the covenant of prosperity. Throughout the Bible, every time the kings remembered the covenant they were blessed, but every time they forgot it they were cursed and became poor. In 1 Corinthians 11:25, we are reminded to invoke the covenant through the Lord's Supper, which is an expression of remembering our commitment to God. Therefore, if you aspire to be a Kingdom Millionaire, honour God's covenant and millions in wealth will come into your life in measures you have never imagined before.

25. *The law of confession*

The law of confession is one of the most powerful ways in which you can be instantly catapulted into the realm of millionaires as you begin to talk your way to the top. By definition, "confession" refers to the prophetic declaration, proclamation, pronunciation and utterance of God's word with a view to effecting changes in our situations and circumstances by the use of our tongue. In a practical sense, it means speaking forth the word of God from the depths of our spirits with the intent to change the prevailing situation

Spiritual Laws & Principles of The Kingdom

and circumstances and to produce the results the word of God talks about. The word "confession" comes from the Greek word *homologous,* which means confessing the word of God. The word *homo* means same and *logos* means the word of God. *Homologous* therefore means confessing with the words of our mouth or saying exactly the same words that God says. The Bible declares in Proverbs 18:21 that *death and life are in the power of the tongue.* This means that confession is a powerful creative force, which can either catapult a man to the highest realms and dimensions of prosperity or degrade a man to the depths of failure.

It is important to highlight that if you want to be a millionaire, you need to start confessing that you are a millionaire, thinking like a millionaire, behaving like a millionaire, speaking like a millionaire and preparing to manage your millions. This is because with God nothing is ever impossible and no word from God will be without power or impossible to fulfil (Luke 1:37) *(Amplified Version).* In other words, God's word contains enough power within itself to cause it to come to pass. Therefore, declaring God's word alone is enough to make one a millionaire. God's word doesn't need help in attaining any more power than it already has. This is because God's words are containers; they contain the ability of God to cause the natural to become *supernatural* and make impossibilities *possible.* The Bible proclaims in Proverbs 18:20 that a man's stomach will be satisfied from the fruit of his mouth. This implies that the fruit of your mouth will satisfy your daily needs, food and prosperity. Therefore, since you can only receive what you confess in the realm of prosperity, talking is very important because your words will reap a harvest. Philosophically speaking, your mouth rules in the realm of prosperity, since prosperity depends on what you say. If you want prosperity, then sow the right words and your words will go forth and reap a harvest. Don't speak your circumstances; instead, speak words that are in line with the word of God.

Words were not made primarily for communication purposes; that is secondary. Instead, words were given specifically to release creative power in your spirit, which is power to create wealth. In essence, words are God's method of operation by which He accomplishes His will, purpose and desire. Words set spiritual laws in motion, such as the law of sin and death and the law of the Spirit of life in Christ Jesus. Words are the most important things in the universe. Philosophically speaking, faith-filled words will tide you over while fear-filled words will defeat you. Words are spiritual containers that carry power. Words are seeds sown with your mouth that produce their own kind. Words are the process starters of life. Words are the building blocks with which you construct your life and future. Words set the cornerstones of your life. Words set boundaries, which confine or release you. Words program the human spirit for success or failure. Words have creative ability. They create the realities you see. God's word—the incorruptible seed – has within it the ability and DNA to cause itself to come to pass. This means that God's word has potency to produce what it talks about. Just by speaking God's word alone is enough to turn around the situation. In Luke 7:6-7 the centurion pleaded with Jesus saying, *"I do not even think of myself worthy to come to you but say the word and my servant will be healed"*. Note that the centurion wasn't asking Jesus to say just anything; instead he was asking Him to speak God's word to turn around his situation. In today's terms, what the centurion was saying is, *"Lord, your word is just enough to change my situation"* and because He took God at His word, he was labelled as the one with the greatest faith in Israel – simply because he believed in confessing God's word. Faith could therefore be best described as speaking God's word with intent to change situations and circumstances.

Concerning the power of confession, Jesus declares in Mark 11:23, *"If you say to a mountain be thou removed and be cast into the sea and you do not doubt but believe that those things which you say shall come to pass, then you shall have whatever you say."* This implies that if you don't say it, then you cannot have it. If you can't confess that you are a millionaire, then you cannot be one. But why is it that people are confessing the word but they are not seeing the fullness of the manifestation of God's blessings in their lives? It is because their confession is devoid of faith, clouded with unbelief and wrong motives, and is not in line with God's will. If you confess the word of God and speak it forth into a situation and it doesn't work out or produce the desired results, of what the word talks about, this means that it was never faith in the first place; it was just presumption. The Bible further declares in Proverbs 18:21 that *death and life are in the power of the tongue and those who love it shall eat of its fruits*. This is talking about prosperity because prosperity is a fruit of our lips. If you keep talking about your needs and not your supply, you will only harvest needs. Any Christian whose life is overwhelmed with lack is certainly harvesting his or her negative confessions. If you are wondering why God doesn't give you a breakthrough in your life, just check how your mouth operates. Many people would readily pay huge sums of money to get a solution to their problems, not realising that the solution is right under their noses; in their mouths. If only you could get a grip on the words that come out of your mouth, you could chart your course for a prosperous life in Christ. Therefore, pertaining to the miracle of supernatural financial provision, your responsibility is to speak God's word to a situation and God's part will be miraculously to release

Spiritual Laws & Principles of The Kingdom

the hundredfold return.

The greater truth is that the word of God, conceived in the heart and spoken from the mouth, becomes a spiritual force that releases faith— which is the creative ability of God. Words establish strongholds, break habits, change things and redirect thought patterns. Words point you in whatever direction they are aimed and released. Words set the course of your life. Words determine your future, your health, your wealth and your place in eternity—you are the prophet of your own life. Words arrive at your future before you do. Words create desires and transmit images that you will eventually live out. Words frame your world. Words spoken today become a living reality tomorrow. Words give permission and licence to spiritual forces to work for you or against you. Words can turn around any situation. Words make demands on the blessing or the curse—whichever you call for. Words are goal setters that give direction and establish destination. Words are our method of operation, by which God accomplishes His will, purpose and desire for our lives.

In the realm of the Spirit, words are pictures and pictures are words. As you speak something into existence, it comes right before you as a picture. There is an intricate connection between prosperity and our confession, which is the fruit of our lips. Every time Jesus is mentioned in the scriptures as a high priest, confession is also mentioned. Paul says in Hebrews 3:1,

"Therefore brethren and partakers of the heavenly calling I beseech you in view of God's mercy to consider Jesus the apostle and high priest of our confession."

Jesus is the high priest who handles our confessions or sacrifices just as in Old Testament days high priests handled animal sacrifices. In the New Testament, Jesus is our high priest, who handles our sacrifices of the word. Paul says in Hebrews 4:14, *"Seeing that we have a great high priest let's hold fast to our confession."* In his capacity as a high priest, Jesus ensures that whatever we confess in line with His word, comes to pass. He will cause all heavenly forces to work on our behalf so that the word of God will not fall onto the ground without bearing fruit. That means your words are backed with divine power from above. Your part is to hold on to your confession. It is therefore evident that if you are a negative talker, you can never be prosperous. When you say that *I can do all things through Christ*, you imply that your wisdom, your strength, your success and your prosperity come from Jesus and that you are elevated into the realm of God's superabundance.

There is evidence in Proverbs 10:20, 12:18, 15:4 and 18:21, that confession is undeniably one of the most integral and significant spiritual exercises that connect humanity with the wealth available in Heaven's storehouse. The greater truth is that words are the answer to every predicament in which a man can find himself going through life. As a matter of fact, there is nothing on this earth so great or so powerful, including the physical body, which cannot be turned around by our words. You can turn around any situation with your words. Even death can be reversed by words; that is why the Bible says death and life are in the power of the tongue. The entire course of nature and the circumstances surrounding every human being are controlled by that person's words. We don't have a choice whether or not we live by words. We do, however, have a choice of what words we live by. If your mouth will feed your heart the word of faith when you don't need it— your heart will feed your mouth the word of faith when you do need it. We appropriate what is ours in Christ by making God's word a daily part of our vocabulary. We are to confess what we can do in Christ, who we are in Christ and what we have in Christ.

Paul further declares in Hebrews 10:23, "*Let us hold fast the profession [confession] of our faith without wavering for Jesus the high priest of our confession.*" Whatever we confess, Jesus and the angels are obligated to bring the confession to pass. That is why Jesus is said to be the high priest of our confession because He handles all our confessions in Heaven. We make our living with our mouth; we don't make our living with our job and that's the problem with a lot of people, who are still trying to make a living by their jobs. Going from pay cheque to pay cheque has, to this point, proven insufficient for achieving everything God has called you to do because you have been trying to make your living the wrong way. Your job is just how you get your seed; your mouth is how you make your living. In the spirit realm we rule over spiritual subject by our vocalising.

Therefore, talk God's word. Keep God's word in your mouth at all times. Keep saying it, don't stop talking it. Keep confessing the word. The Bible declares in Deuteronomy 6:6-9 in the NIV Version: *These commandments that I give you today are to be on your hearts. Impress them on your children. Talk about them when you sit at home and when you walk along the road, when you lie down and when you get up. Tie them as symbols on your hands and bind them on your foreheads. Write them on the doorframes of your houses and on your gates.* This means that speaking God's word is supposed to be our culture, our second nature and that which absorbs all our consciousness. According to Deuteronomy 11:18-21, the result of speaking the word is that *your days may be multiplied, and the days of your children, in the land which the Lord swore unto your fathers to give them, as the days of heaven upon earth.* There is no problem on this earth so great and so powerful that it cannot be turned around with words of faith. The entire course of nature—your future and destiny, success and prosperity—is controlled by the words you speak.

26. *The law of meditation*

The law of meditation is to a large extent connected to the law of visualisation because both are twin processes of soul prosperity. The reason why many people do not see a manifestation of Heaven's wealth is because their thinking is wrong, faulty and not in line with the word of God. Philosophically speaking, if your thinking is wrong, then your believing is going to be wrong and if your believing is wrong, then your talking is going to be wrong. Therefore you have got to get all three of them — your thinking, your believing, and your speaking – synchronised with the Word of God. It is easy to act on God's word if you have been speaking the word and meditating on the word. Hence, meditation should not be used in isolation but in conjunction with other spiritual exercises. That is why Kenneth Copeland says that *Meditation on the Word enlarges our capacity for faith; it transforms and expands our capacity to believe and receive.* Often, people memorise scriptures, but that is not enough. They memorise verses, but they don't spend enough time with those verses for them to become real—for those verses to become Spirit and life (John 6:63)—to their spirit. This suggests that meditation is highly imperative action in financial prosperity. Meditation is God's recipe for boundless prosperity and phenomenal success. It is the secret to a victorious, successful and prosperous life. This is because the measure of attention you give to the Word will determine the extent of your prosperity in life. If you pay greater attention to the Word, you function with a greater degree of revelation knowledge which will propel your life forward and catapult you into the realm of millionaires.

In the context of this revelation, "meditation" refers to the process of conceiving, visualising, absorbing and assimilating the word of God into the human spirit so as to release its creative power to change life situations and circumstances involving lack, poverty and debt. In a practical sense, meditation is done through silently talking the word, reading the word, memorising the word or thinking the word. Joshua 1:8 unveils God's tested and guaranteed recipe for unending prosperity.

In this regard, Moses strongly cautioned his spiritual son Joshua, saying,

Apostle Frequency Revelator

"Do not let this book of law depart from your mouth but meditate day and night that you may be careful to do according to all that is written in it, then your prosperity shall break forth like the brightness at noon day."

Note that in the context of this spiritual command, there is a condition attached to prosperity and that condition is the meditation process, that in order for a person to proper, he must start by meditating on the word of God. This means that prosperity is born out of the meditation process. Meditation is the creative force or power of the human mind. It is a conception process. As the word of God becomes permanently embedded in your mind, spirit and entire system, prosperity becomes a reality. As you meditate on God's word, the word is seasoned in your spirit such that you think, talk and live the Word. The Bible shows this to us as the way to make your way prosperous. When admonishing his spiritual son, Timothy, in (1 Timothy 4.15), the Apostle Paul in 1 Timothy 4.15, reiterated the same truth: *"Meditate upon these things, give thyself wholly to them; that thy profiting may appear to all"*. This means that when you meditate on God's word, your prosperity, progress, advancement and success will spread abroad and be evident for all to see. This is God's divine road map for true and lasting prosperity. It must be understood that the realm of the Spirit works on the basis of pictures, codes and visions; as we meditate on these pictures, our visions become a reality. This implies that part of your journey to becoming a Kingdom Millionaire involves directing your focus on God's word as well as receiving a flood of revelations from God's word. This is because everything you would ever need for a prosperous life is wrapped up in God's word, which is an infallible manual for a successful, victorious and prosperous life. The only material given to you to build your millions is God's word; hence to ignore God's word is to set one's self up for extreme disadvantage in life. However, to set yourself up for a life of superabundance, you must have a rapacious appetite for the word of God and be a *Word practitioner* by doing what it says and then amassing millions in wealth will not be a problem at all.

It is a greater truth that without a revelation you cannot become a millionaire because becoming a millionaire is a revelation of God's financial wealth. You, therefore, need to catch a revelation of what God says about prosperity, and then you will walk into your millions. Revelation is the opposite of ignorance. Many people have not received from God because they are ignorant of what God says about their situation and about how to become a Kingdom Millionaire. It is, therefore, a greater truth that prosperity has to touch the realm of your souls; as John declared in 3 John 1:2: *"brethren I I wish above all things that you could prosper* **as your soul prospers**." This implies that you will not be able to receive financial prosperity without soul prosperity. And in this context John is talking about the supply of all that he needs in the bodily realm. The prerequisite is that you prosper and nourish your soul first. Igniting the fire of God in your soul through the meditation process is what will make your prosperity break forth like the brightness of noonday. As your soul prospers, so will your body and spirit. Against this background, therefore, if you want to prosper, you have to deal with your circumstances, thought life and what your thoughts meditate on and contemplate. This is because your thought life is such a vital aspect of the law of prosperity. It has to be controlled and subjected to the word of God. Hence, meditation plays a fundamental role in making your vision of becoming a millionaire a reality. This is why you cannot receive these things (*revelations on prosperity*) just because I tell you about them. Instead, you must constantly and persistently meditate on them until they become real to you and an integral part of your life. In a practical sense, you have to take the scriptures on prosperity and meditate on them until they become a reality in your heart, until you know that prosperity belongs to you. Once you have a revelation of divine prosperity in your spirit, you won't allow Satan to take it from you and it won't be long before your millions break forth as a visible and tangible manifestation in the natural realm. Moreover, the Bible declares in Psalm 1:1-3:

> *Blessed is the man that walketh not in the counsel of the ungodly, nor standeth in the way of sinners, nor sitteth in the seat of the scornful. But his delight is in the law of the Lord; and in his law doth he meditate day and night. And he shall be like a tree planted by the rivers of water, that bringeth forth his fruit in his season; his leaf also shall not wither; and whatsoever he doeth shall prosper.*

This implies that meditation is the only spiritual exercise that guarantees automatic prosperity. In other words, the minute you start meditating on God's word, prosperity is bound to break forth like the surging waters of the sea. As shown in this scripture, God has already given a verdict that *whatsoever you do shall prosper* hence your prosperity is God ordained. Therefore refuse to struggle in life, for success and prosperity are in your spirit. But the question is: How do I meditate on God's word in a practical sense? The answer to this is simple. Apply the word to you personally. Allow the Holy Spirit to make the word a reality in your heart. Develop a voracious appetite for God's word and carefully ponder how this word applies to your life. Dwell on how the word changes your situation. Place yourself in agreement with what the word says about you. See yourself as God sees you. Realise the integrity in God's word and cultivate a personal culture of studying and pondering over God's word. If you do these things, it won't be long before your millions break forth and manifest in your bank account.

27. The law of visualisation/imagination

This is one of the integral spiritual principles of tapping into the realm of possessing God's abundant wealth. It suffices in this regard to break the ice by saying that millions in wealth doesn't usually come by accident; instead, one must first visualise or see them in the Spirit before their manifestation in the physical realm. There is no such thing as an accidental millionaire. It is a spiritual fact that the realm of the Spirit operates on the basis of pictures and symbols. Dreams are pictures of impossibilities imparted into our spirits. Your vision starts as a picture implanted in your spirit and, as you water or nurture it through the word, it becomes clearer than before. For you to receive millions, you must therefore have a vision where you actually see them in the Spirit first and, when that vision has grown in you as you visualise and conceptualise it, it then breaks forth in the natural. Therefore, you must see yourself being a millionaire, owning mansions, walking in abundance, financing the work of ministry, sponsoring Kingdom visions and projects even when you don't have a cent in your pocket. The principle is that you have to see it before you can have it. When I use the word "see," I'm not talking about seeing with your physical eyes. I'm talking about seeing with the eye of faith or with your spirit man, the man on the inside. In 2 Kings 2, the prophet Elijah says to Elisha:

"If you see me when I go, you can have my mantle or anointing."

The Lord is saying to us, *"If you can see it, you can have it."* By the same token, if you see millions in wealth with the eyes of your faith, you already have them and it won't be long before they can break forth as a visible and tangible manifestation in the natural realm.

Visualisation or imagination is therefore *the ability and capacity to see into the spirit dimension beyond the realm of the senses.* The greater truth is that God has given you the power to imagine things. It is therefore imperative that you train the eyes of your understanding so that you are able to see freely in the spirit dimension and the flow of ideas that comes into your spirit will enable you to see a bigger picture. The ability to imagine will lead you to see ample opportunities all around you. You must therefore not make your mind blank and potentially prone to demonic thoughts; instead, you need to imagine your millions in wealth before you can possess them. In the context of this revelation, as much as money is physical, it is also spiritual; hence, you need to imagine it. Spiritual things need to be tapped into or pulled down. This means that imagination pulls down spiritual things from the realm of the Spirit into reality. There is power in imagination. In actual fact, everything in life came into being or existence due to the power of imagination. This is what I call *God's creative power. The question is: What do you see?* Some people only see their failures, weaknesses and all sorts of unproductive things; hence, they are not able to prosper. Whatever you see in the Spirit is what determines what you get. Whatever you imagine will surely become reality. Many people wish for things like cars, houses and property but they lack the power of imagination, which means that these things never come their way. You must see these things first in the realm of the Spirit before you receive them in the natural realm. The greater truth is that only people with the right imagination can draw a pool of money or tap into their future to acquire things. Therefore, keep imagining how rich and great you are; see your dreams coming true, your position and bright future. The principle is that as long as you can imagine, the universe will grant you the right access into the realm of millionaires. While money doesn't grow on trees, it can be developed in your imagination. As a new creation, you have an extraordinary capacity to contemplate, envision and see endless possibilities. There are things you might have desired and prayed about; take hold of them with your spirit and they will be yours.

In the realm of God's prosperity, the extent to which you are able to see or visualise your millions in wealth in the Spirit will determine how much you can receive from God. For example, when God took Moses to the highest mountain and caused him to survey the whole land of Canaan, He said to him, *"As far as your eyes can see, that I have given to you."* This means that the number of blessings or millions in wealth that you receive from God will to a large extent be determined by your ability to visualise them in the spirit realm. Why does God want us to see our millions in the Spirit first before their manifestation in the physical? This is because, in the realm of the Spirit, blessings are possessed through vision. The moment you see something, you possess it. In the realm of the Spirit, something becomes yours because you have seen it. In a related incident narrated in Genesis 15:5, God took Abraham outside and showed him the stars in the sky and told him that his descendants would be as many as the stars. This is because God knew that there would be times when, in the natural, it would seem as if the vision would not come to pass but if the vision were implanted in Abraham's imagination, it would propel him to move forward. Before God could use Isaiah mightily, He had to show him a vision first (Jeremiah 1:11); He then asked him a rhetorical question, "*Son of man, what do you see?*" This is because God is interested more than anything else in the size of your vision because how big your vision is will determine how far you can go with God. God can go as far as the size of your vision because not only does the word of God get assimilated into your spirit but it also gets assimilated into your mind. Hence, the more you see the image, the more the image becomes permanently engraved in your spirit. Therefore, if you aspire to become a millionaire, then you must see yourself as a millionaire and start behaving or acting like one. Sooner or later you will be catapulted into that realm. When you focus more on training your imagination through God's word, you will see what other men don't see; you will find yourself living in a realm that the world doesn't think is real; an arena they probably only dream of. You will see millions of wealth when everybody is only seeing lack and hardship.

The law of visualisation is like conception. Before a baby is brought forth into the world, she goes through conception. Then there is a gestation period where the baby grows and develops and, once the baby has grown big enough, she is born. The difference is that, with regard to financial laws, the time frame is not the same; it can be shorter or longer. Note that God does not give you a vision first then after that a provision; instead, He gives you a provision or abundance first then after that a vision. That is why it is not fair to judge a person who is undergoing spiritual transformation as not being prosperous because they may be going through a transformation phase. This person may have something done to them because they are living right with God and you are looking at the sketch not the final work. For example, when an artist is painting a first few sketches, a work of art may look like a horrible thing. But wait until the art is finished, then you will see that the end is beautiful. You may be looking at a scratch not the end of the painting. The sketch is undergoing processing; it is a work in progress. Gold is the most precious substance in the universe but if you were to look at it in its early stage as it is exhumed from the earth, you would judge it and say it looks horrible. But wait until it is purified or has undergone purification in fire. It comes out as clear and glittering as the morning star. Millionaires are produced in the same way. This is why many people who are destined to become millionaires face rejection from the world during their early days because the world does not see anything of value in them until their millions finally manifest. This is why you must not worry at all about your present circumstances and how you live now or how people judge you because you might be a millionaire in the making and the world is not even aware of it. Therefore, do not give up when it appears under your present life circumstances that you might never become a millionaire. You might be undergoing training or in the process of being shaped into a millionaire. This is how you might eventually become a Kingdom Millionaire in this end-time season.

28. The law of righteousness

There is an intricate connection between prosperity and the law of righteousness, which means right living with God. Contrary to how some religious folks have stigmatised the concept, righteousness is not conforming to some form of godliness but it's an impartation of the nature of God in our spirits, producing in us the rightness of God and the ability to do what is right all the time and to stand in the presence of God without any condemnation, guilt or inferiority. Righteousness is such a powerful, alluring magnetic force because money always follows righteousness. This means that as a new creation, you are the demonstration or the quintessence of God's righteousness; hence money, wealth or riches are naturally attracted to you. Righteousness is not based on what one has done or not done but on who God is. It is an expression of the Spirit, as God declares in Jeremiah 31:33 and Colossians 2:14 that *He shall write His laws in our hearts.* Jesus said in Matthew 6:33): "*Seek ye first the kingdom of God and its righteousness and all these things will be added to you.*" This means that prosperity comes when you prioritise or put the things of God above natural things or demands and then programme your mind in such a way that you constantly seek to extend the Kingdom of God and do the things of God in the exact way He wants them to be done. This implies that you start by prospering spiritually first before your prosperity can break forth in the physical realm. If you dwell on the things of God, you become like a magnet that attracts those things to you. All you need to do is take care of the business of God and He will take care of all your needs. The people of the world spend time seeking after food, shelter and clothes and in the process neglect the weightier matters of the word of God and their spiritual life. The Bible declares in Psalms 1:1 that *blessed is a man who walks not in the counsel of the ungodly nor stands in the way of sinners but whose delight is in the Lord. He shall be like a tree planted by many rivers, whose leaf does not wither,* **whatever he does prospers.**

Apostle Frequency Revelator

This implies that prosperity comes through righteous standing with God. As you sanctify and set yourself apart and distinguish yourself in such a way that you do not mingle with or entertain sin in any way, your righteousness will break forth like perennial rivers of long-lasting prosperity and trigger an abundant manifestation of God's blessings over your life.

The Bible presents an incident in Samuel 4:1-11 in which Israel went to war against the Philistines and they were defeated. They decided to bring back the Ark of the Covenant into their camp but, because they were not living right, they lost more battles. But when you are in righteousness, you seek to bring back the Ark to the lost souls around the world, to rule and reign over life, city, nation and world. And if you do that, all your needs will be met. 2 Samuel 7:1-7 records how David wanted to build a house for the Ark of God. He wanted God to be blessed. He sought the Kingdom of God first and wanted God to have the best. This story implies that if you build God's house, God will build you houses. He will take care of all your things if you take care of His house, His Kingdom and things of the Kingdom. The Bible declares in 2 Corinthians 9:11 that *he who supplies the seed to the sower and bread for food, supplies and multiplies the seed you have sown and increases the fruit of your righteousness.* **Righteousness produces prosperity;** hence, if you live a righteous life, prosperity will find itself in you. In Genesis 39:1, Joseph was given a chance to commit fornication with Potiphar's wife but he chose to live righteously. Don't blame your circumstances; if you live righteously, God will cause you to prosper, anywhere, anytime, anyplace.

In 1 Timothy 4:8, the Bible proclaims that *bodily exercise profits a little but godliness profits in all things having the promise of life that now is and what is to come.* This implies that if you live righteously you will reap profits both in this earthly realm and in Heaven. In Proverbs 10:3, the Bible says *the Lord will not allow a righteous soul to famish but He cast away the desires of the wicked.* This implies that you could be thrown somewhere in a dark place to starve but God will be with you. Proverbs 11:28 declares that *he who trusts in his riches shall fall but the righteous shall flourish like foliage.* This implies that the righteous will flourish wherever they are planted, just like Joseph was planted in a place where no one would expect prosperity but he flourished to the extent of becoming the topranked man in the Egyptian government. Daniel was taken as a slave boy and no one would have expected a slave to prosper but he rose up to be the King's right-hand man in the whole Kingdom of Babylon. Moreover, the Bible says in Proverbs 13:21 that *evil pursues sinners but to the righteous, good shall be repaid.* This implies that if you live righteously, you are on God's payroll and he will be paying you. Proverbs 13:25 says that *the righteous eats to the satisfying*

Spiritual Laws & Principles of The Kingdom

of his soul but the stomach of the wicked shall be in want. This means that if you live righteously, you shall eat and eat until you are satisfied and have abundance. It therefore suffices to adjudicate on the basis of scriptural evidence that righteousness breeds prosperity and provokes an unprecedented stream of God's blessings on an individual.

29. The law of faith

In an endeavour to bring forth a revelation of what faith is and its connection to the law of prosperity, let me start by explaining what faith is not. There is a difference between faith and presumption, or optimism, since these are aspects of human nature. Many people are actually optimistic and presumptuous and they tend to mistake these things for faith. This is the reason why they are not seeing the fullness of the manifestation of God's blessings in their lives. If you confess the word of God and speak it forth into a situation and it doesn't work out or produce the results it promises, then it means that it was never faith in the first place; it was just presumption or optimism.

In essence, faith is the mind of God revealed to man so that he can operate and have dominion in the dimensions of time, space and matter. It is the divine ability given to man to go beyond the natural realm. Faith allows us to cross the limits of the natural realm and venture into the dimension of eternity. Faith is a force that allows us to cross over the barriers of time, space and matter and exit our natural realm that makes us subject to the senses. Moreover, faith is a force that brings forth our blessings from the spirit realm to the natural realm. It must be expressly understood that blessings are released in the Spirit but the channel through or means by which they are brought to manifestation in the natural realm is faith. That is why God declared in Hebrews 11:6 that *without faith it is impossible to please God* and by the same token without faith it is impossible to receive from God because if you can't please God then you can receive from Him. Therefore, you need faith to please God and you need faith to receive from God. It is a fact that no one can bankrupt God's supply. Whatever you claim from Him and whatever you believe God for, you receive it based on your faith. Faith is what allows God to deliver His divine provision or supernaturally to bring into the natural realm the resources we need. Faith converts things that cannot be seen into something certain, tangible and real. Faith plays a pivotal role in prosperity because God cannot bless you unless you give Him something to use to bless you through. In other words, you need to give God your faith to work with.

Apostle Frequency Revelator

In the realm of prosperity, faith causes our blessings or millions in wealth to manifest speedily by breaking the laws of space and time. It must be expressly understood that God does not live in the realm of time; instead, He lives in the realm of eternity. Hence, from God's standpoint, everything is complete and in the past tense. It is a greater truth, therefore, that God started creating us in eternity and finished us long before giving us the shape and form we have today. Long before you came on the scene, God deposited great reserves of treasure for you in this world. Ephesians 3:8 describes it as *unsearchable riches- inexhaustible wealth*. What you ought to do is simply discover what belongs to you in Christ. All we need to do in the present time is to claim, command and appropriate our millions in wealth by faith in the now. We make plans according to faith not time. If we operate according to the natural realm, it takes a considerable amount of time for our blessings to manifest in the physical. Hence, faith breaks the law of time and causes our blessings to manifest speedily in the now. By faith we can determine the exact time to receive our blessings. This is because these things have already been done in the Spirit and are waiting for us to decide when we are going to claim them. The realities of our heavenly kingdom are activated through faith, acknowledgement and proclamation. Therefore boldly proclaim that you are who God says you are, you have what He says you have and you can do what He says you can, and millions in wealth shall stream in your direction.

It is an irrefutable fact that faith is the past and the future together in the present, constituting the now. The reason that many people are not seeing the full manifestation of the wealth of God is because they live too much in the future; yet, God lives in the now. Faith is not in the future because faith is not going to be; faith is now. Faith compresses time and causes the future to invade the present. Most believers know where they come from and where they are going but few believe what they are now. This is an error because God declares the end from the beginning, meaning that He finishes something before showing man in the beginning. In other words, God finishes tasks in eternity first, and then He takes man on a journey to fulfil what He has already completed in eternity. As far as God is concerned, the past, present and future are all in the past tense.

In the context of prosperity, money is only a tool to get all the things you want and where money isn't enough to get them, you can still obtain them by faith.

Your purchasing power isn't money, but faith. It is a currency of Heaven and a passport for parading in the spirit realm to get hold of our spiritual blessings. Therefore in your quest to amass humungous wealth from Heaven, believe that you are a millionaire and before long, your millions shall break forth in the natural realm.

It is a greater truth that the dimension of faith is not revealed to the senses. When God commands us to do something, it might not make sense because the carnal mind cannot see the invisible. When we take our measure of faith to the limit, God takes us to a higher level. This means that when nothing new is happening in church, then our faith has stopped growing. Hence, we need revelation to break into or pave a way into a new dimension. The level of revelation in an individual determines the measure of faith by which he will operate. According to the word of God in Romans 1:17, we move from one dimension of faith to another. Faith is a constant movement; it is not stagnant, for the Christian life was never designed to stay at one level. It is a constant migration from glory to glory and from faith to faith as proclaimed in 2 Corinthians 3:18. This indicates that the movement does not begin at a point of departure but it takes off from a place that is already advanced. Faith is therefore one such powerful force that can invade the realm of the Spirit to bring forth into physical manifestation millions in Heaven's wealth and riches. That is why a man of great faith is a man of great wealth because it takes great faith to manifest great wealth.

30. *The law of sacrifice*

The law of sacrifice states that the level of sacrifice that an individual is willing to offer is what determines the level, degree, intensity and gravity of the manifestation of Heaven's common wealth of blessings. At times we need to make extraordinary sacrifices to receive extraordinary things from God. Jesus attested to this spiritual truth in Mark 10:28-30 when Peter said to him, *"See, we have given up everything, and come after you."*

In response, Jesus said,

> *"Truly I say to you, there is no man who has given up house, or brothers, or sisters, or mother, or father, or children, or land, because of me and the good news, who will not get a hundred times as much now in this time, houses, and brothers, and sisters, and mothers, and children, and land—though with great troubles; and, in the world to come, eternal life."*

This is the basis of the law of sacrifice. The heart that sacrifices receives abundant provision in return. This is why God sacrificed His only begotten son and in return, after His resurrection from the dead, God received many sons to His glory.

Sacrifice may not necessarily take the form of a financial sacrifice as some pastors have overemphasised, but may rather be a sacrifice of time, energy, work or property. Sacrifice can move God's hand and cause Him to do something unusual on behalf of humanity. In Esther 3:5-6, Haman understood the power of this principle and made an effort to apply it in a negative direction by seeking to pay a lump sum of money in order to annihilate the whole tribe of Israel. The Bible records another incident in 2 Kings 3:27, when the Israelites pursued their enemies in, the King sacrificed his only son and this culminated in indignation in the camp of the Israelites. This implies that huge sacrifices are taken notice of in the realm of the Spirit; hence, some people will receive much just because they sacrificed more to receive. This is a biblical principle where people receive from God as a result of sacrifice. It grants people who would have gone the extra mile to make humungous sacrifices to receive from God as a result of their sacrifice. While in the New Testament we don't sacrifice with the blood of goats and bulls, we still sacrifice through consecration, holiness, worship and fasting. If you have fasted, prayed and done everything in your ability but find that situations are not changing, then resort to giving a sacrifice such as you have never given before in your life and an alarming breakthrough will come speedily. This is why, when David was offered a field freely to offer sacrifices after the angel withdrew his sword in Jerusalem, David refused and said, *"I will not offer anything that will cost me nothing."* This is because it must cost you something to sacrifice to the Lord something of value or the best you have in both your heart and mind. Sacrifice is therefore a channel, or pipeline by which unusual blessings of God are released upon humanity.

While it is true that by the grace of God we receive things freely from Him, it is also a greater truth that anything that leaves the hand of God to manifest in the realm of the natural comes through sacrifice. The anointing, the glory, the mantle and the presence all come through sacrifice. It's just that at times, when we receive something from the realm of the Spirit, we may not be conscious of the fact that we have made certain sacrifices to receive it. This is because a lot of sacrifices are made behind the scenes in the invisible realm; for example, through seeking the Lord in fasting and prayer, meditation, high levels of concentration and a complete devotion to the word of God.

Spiritual Laws & Principles of The Kingdom

In essence, to meet God and receive from Him requires sacrifice. Many people just go to a place where the presence of God is moving but they can't receive anything because they have not sacrificed anything to stay in the presence. In Exodus 19:10, when God wanted to manifest Himself to the Israelites in the wilderness, He commanded Moses to tell the Israelites to consecrate themselves for three days so that He would appear. In other words, this was a sacrifice that qualified them to enter into His presence. And *God demands that no man should appear in his presence empty handed* (Deuteronomy 16:16; Exodus 23:17). That is another sacrifice. In short God was saying that no one should come before Him without a sacrifice. This could be in the form of an unusual act of giving, or pursuing a risky business opportunity, or making huge investments. Millionaires are not scared to take a risk; instead they are propelled by the power of faith to invest in millions. Immediately after God created man, He instructed Cain and Abel to make sacrifices to Him and this shows how vital the act of sacrifice is to Him. On the basis of scriptural evidence, it therefore suffices to conclude that if you want to tap into the realm of millionaires speedily, then make huge spiritual or financial sacrifices and millions will chase after you.

31. The law of divine transaction and spiritual exchange

It is of paramount importance to highlight that in the realm of God's prosperity, there are certain blessings that a man can never receive directly from the hand of God. At times, God deposits a wealth of His blessings on a certain man of God who has paid a price through sacrifices, which then qualifies him to receive abundantly from God's presence because *God is a rewarder of those who diligently seek him* (Hebrews 11:6). God then expects the majority of believers to make spiritual withdrawals from and divine transactions of His blessings with those anointed men to whom He has imparted a wealth of His blessings. This is done through a sub-spiritual principle of divine transaction and exchange called *placing a demand*. "Placing a demand" means expressing a deep desire or hunger for supernatural manifestation. According to the law of divine transaction, some blessings are transferred, exchanged or transacted in the realm of the Spirit even without a word being spoken or people noticing. A demand is placed by faith, in which those who desire to receive God's blessings tap into God's spiritual laws and principles to claim and receive what God has imparted to His servants. This implies that you may not necessarily receive your wealth directly from God but that you receive it from a man of God through impartation or placing a demand for those blessings. Identifying the source of God's blessings and acknowledging the blessing or anointing on the servants of God is a vital key to receiving from a man of God. To receive abundantly from a man of God in this way, one must identify the mantle, honour the mantle, serve the mantle and then receive from the mantle.

This spiritual law is connected to the law of giving and receiving. However, it is important to highlight that some of these spiritual laws are manipulated by the demonic realm. For example, through the law of divine exchange and spiritual transactions, some sacrifices are made by agents of Satan and covenants are created even without people knowing. Decrees and curses on people's lives are issued and they take effect or pre-eminence through these laws. This is the same principle that the devil tapped into when he manipulated and stole the world from Adam. When Adam sinned, there was a transaction that took place in the Spirit, which automatically demanded that he hand over authority to rule the world to the devil. In Jesus's office in Heaven, He receives many petitions from the devil against His people for their wrongdoing. When Jesus told Peter that Satan demanded for him, it was not just idle talk but a revelation of this spiritual reality. And *the Lord said, "Simon, Simon! Indeed, Satan has asked for you, that he may sift you as wheat"* (Luke 22:31). Satan had legal grounds to place a demand or to petition Jesus for the right to sift Peter like wheat because he had denied the Lord three times. This is because when you sin, it gives the devil a legal foothold over your life and opens the door for the enemy to take possession and control of your blessings. This is how so many believers have lost their blessings because they were intercepted and manipulated, exchanged and twisted in the spirit world by high-ranking demons responsible for spiritual wickedness. But why does God allow our blessings to be manipulated in this way? This is because God is a God of rules. He too has to observe rules. There is only one way for Jesus to help, and that is the way of grace. When you pray the prayer for grace, God can then give you grace and deliver you.

At the extreme end, a positive spiritual transaction took place when Jesus was crucified on the cross and when He resurrected from the dead. A divine exchange was ordained at the cross, where every wicked thing produced by our rebellion was placed on Jesus and all the goodness in Him became ours because of His obedience. On the cross, God placed all the consequences of the world's iniquity, guilt, shame and rebellion on Jesus's shoulders. Through the law of divine exchange, Jesus was whipped so that you could receive healing; He was made poor so that you could be rich; and He took your grief and sorrow on the cross so that you could receive joy and abundant life. For every negative experience that Jesus went through, there was a corresponding positive transaction that was imparted to your life. In the realm of the Spirit, there was a paradigm shift in the rightful ownership, control, power, rule and possession of the world from the devil to the people. By the same token, in the realm of God's prosperity, there are certain things that we need to do in the Spirit to hand over things or receive things. For example, yielding to the Holy Ghost or living a consecrated life can be instrumental in receiving or provoking a flow of God's blessings. There are so many things that are transacted or exchanged in the realm of the Spirit without our knowing it. In actual fact every word you speak and every action you take in the Spirit is followed by a spiritual transaction. Some positive actions result in the impartation or addition of blessings while other, negative, ones result in a withdrawal or reduction of the blessings. For example, if you sin, a negative transaction takes place, but if you give or commit yourself to the things of God, a positive spiritual transaction results.

The Bible declares in Isaiah 53:4-5 that *Jesus was wounded so that we could be forgiven hence by his stripes, we are healed.* This means that He was whipped in exchange for our healing; He carried our sicknesses and suffered our sorrows so that we could receive healing. He was made poor so that, through His poverty, we might be rich; He became sin and carried our sinful nature so that we could be justified; He died on the cross so that we could share in His eternal life; He carried our curse so that we could be blessed; He suffered our shame so we could partake of His glory and He ultimately suffered rejection so we could be accepted by Him. An understanding of the law of divine transaction can therefore help you to transfer a multitude of wealth from the spirit realm into the physical realm.

32. *The law of divine connectivity and contagious association*

According to the law of divine connectivity, an individual can only receive or partake in spiritual blessings when he is in the Spirit or connected to a spiritual source. This means that to receive spiritual things, you need to receive them while in the Spirit by observing all the laws and properties of the realm of the Spirit. Through the law of divine connectivity, a person can connect himself to the perennial and unending source of God's power and have access to the unlimited blessings of God in the supernatural. The Bible affirms in John 4:24 that *God is a spirit and therefore those who worship Him must do so in truth and in spirit.* By the same token, God is a spirit and those who want to receive anything from a spirit must be in the Spirit because God does not live in the realm of senses but in the realm of the Spirit. Any attempt to receive spiritual things while in the flesh is regarded as carnality and rejected as per the laws of the Spirit. This implies that to partake fully in the fullness of the wealth of God's resources, you must be rightly positioned in the Spirit to receive. For example, if the antenna of a television is not rightly positioned, no signal can be accessed no matter how powerful the television set is. The key is in divine connection. The inflow and outflow of God's financial blessings and resources take place through divine connectivity. This is why Jesus said in John 15:7:

"Abide in me and I will abide in you and if you abide in me then you will ask of me anything and I will give you."

This speaks of a divine connection and it means that the secret or key to receiving your wealth of millions from God is in abiding, which literally speaks of establishing a divine connection to God. How then do we connect ourselves to God? This is possible through fellowship with the Holy Ghost, practising the presence, prayer and fasting, reading the word, meditation and other spiritual exercises.

There is a spiritual frequency with which the blessings of God flow. Connecting yourself to the source of God's blessings is the key to receiving your millions in wealth from Him. Some blessings of God flow through the sphere of influence, association or impartation. The law of contagious experience states that by virtue of affiliation, partnership, networking and relationship with a man whom God has blessed or entrusted with the wealth of His blessings, those blessings can automatically flow or be imparted to the recipient. If you need an anointing for prosperity, for example, connecting yourself to a ministry that excels in that area or putting yourself under a spiritual covering that has tested the goodness of the Lord in the area of financial prosperity will be highly beneficial. Many people have not been able to access the millions in wealth available from God because they are not connected in the realm of the Spirit. I do not intend to create any confusion in the body of Christ but it is a spiritual truth that the ministry where you fellowship is what determines how far you can go with God and the magnitude of the blessings you can receive from Him. In actual fact, the level of revelation of the ministry in which you serve is a key determinant of the depths, heights and proportions of supernatural blessings you can access from God. Therefore, in your journey to becoming a Kingdom Millionaire, connect yourself to the right ministry that is manifesting the fruits of prosperity, and millions shall unreservedly stream in your direction.

33. *The law of divine destiny and purpose*

It is a spiritual truth that all financial prosperity is connected to God's purpose. To a large extent, the purpose for which God brought you to earth will determine the amount of wealth you can receive from God. It must be expressly understood that God takes matters of destiny seriously; hence, His blessings always flow in connection with His divine purpose, destiny and calling. It is of paramount importance to point out that the level of our calling and destiny differs among individuals since some are called to minister to the world through global ministries, some are given regional visions, while some minister at local level. The reality is that the extent of the size of the vision is what will determine the amount of wealth one can receive from God. By the principle of divine purpose, Joseph was made minister in charge of all the wealth of Egypt. Prosperity came because he was destined to save the nation of Israel. It was not for himself only; rather, he was used as a means to bring deliverance to the nation of Israel during a period of great drought. It is a divine truth that God creates destinies. God has a divine destiny for every man but He is not limited by that destiny. Though He created a destiny for man, He reserves the right and ability to create another destiny for the same man. Although this spiritual reality boggles the mind, it's what God has ordained for you; hence there is no limit to what you can be in Christ. That is why it is possible for anybody to become a Kingdom Millionaire in this endtime season.

The greater truth is that the grace to manifest millions in wealth from Heaven often comes when we find our purpose. Therefore, if you want millions in wealth to flood your life swiftly and speedily, simply do what God brought you here on earth to do and millions will follow you. This is the essence of the law of divine destiny and purpose. The reality is that there are people who cry for the anointing, power, miracles, signs and wonders, and finances, but these things never come their way because these people are not following their divine destiny and purpose. If you want to move the hand of God concerning anything, either finances or millions in wealth from Heaven, simply follow your divine destiny and purpose and millions will come. That is the ultimate solution. In actual fact, that is how cases are solved in Heaven. In Heaven, the significance, value or weight of our lives is measured or determined by whether or not we have fulfilled our divine destiny and purpose. Therefore, decisions are made to release millions in wealth to us based on our divine destiny and purpose on earth. If you see someone prospering abundantly, it may not necessarily mean that God loves him more than others, but it could be that the person in question has a greater or weightier purpose that requires that he uses more financial resources than others. So the key here is in purpose and, as a matter of fact, all Heaven's decisions revolve around issues of destiny and purpose. The difference between the wealthy Christian and the poor one lies in their purpose. If you were to check carefully you would find that those people who seem to be prospering financially have found their purpose. True success is to be what God called you to be. If a manufacturer puts a car on the road and it functions according to the manufacturer's specifications, then the car is successful. By the same token, if you discover and pursue what God has called you to do, millions in wealth will unreservedly stream in your direction because money always chases after purpose.

Usually, when God gives you more blessings than usual, those blessings are not yours, spiritually speaking, but they have been given to you for Kingdom purposes. This is why they spill over to cover even those in your immediate sphere of influence, just as Lot was blessed because of Abraham. When you receive more blessings, God is using you as a channel to bring forth these blessings for their intended purpose. That is why God uses people of purpose and vision to receive and dispatch Kingdom wealth because they already understand God's system of operation or provision. In Esther 4:14, Mordecai says to

Esther,

"Who knows whether you have been brought to the kingdom for such a time as this?"

Esther was made to prosper to the extent of being made the wife of the king because God had the nation of Israel in mind. This means that when God prospers you, there are millions of people across the globe who He has in mind and He wants to touch or bless them through your prosperity. This is because God's prosperity is always connected to a particular destiny.

Spiritual Laws & Principles of The Kingdom

That is why Paul proclaims in Philippians 4:19 that *the Lord supplies all my needs according to the riches in Christ's glory* because the abundance of God's provision is always connected to a specific purpose. In Jeremiah 11:29, God declares that, *"I know the plans that I have for you, plans to prosper you and not to harm you, plans to give you a future."* This implies that, whenever God publicly declares that He will bless someone, His blessings are always connected to his future or the accomplishment of a particular destiny. Therefore, if you want huge financial wealth to manifest in your life, in millions, then connect yourself to the source of prosperity and millions will chase after you.

34. The law of divine increase and catapult-action

The law of divine increase awakens us to a fundamental reality that the life of a believer is programmed to move in one direction only; that is, forward-and-upward. Increase, advancement and growth are what characterise the nature of the system of Kingdom prosperity. In the realm of God's prosperity, we are therefore entitled to a hundredfold increase in wisdom, in knowledge, in revelation, in power, in grace, in speed and in favour. These are the dimensions of God's prosperity revealed in the Bible. In Genesis 26:13 declares that,

> *Isaac the man began to prosper, and he continued to prosper until he became prosperous.*

In other words, the moment you tap into the realm of Kingdom prosperity, a propelling force takes hold of your spirit and propels you forward, accelerates you towards your destiny and ultimately catapults you from one level of blessing to another. It is through the law of increase that the Bible says we move from faith to faith and from glory to glory, from power to power, from wealth to wealth and from millions to millions. Therefore through the revelation of this spiritual principle, it gets us to a place whereby we move from wealth to wealth and from millions to millions. The *law of increase* postulates that we must never become comfortable and remain in one spot for too long no matter the laurels you were decorated with at that level. Instead, you must conquer new grounds, explore new frontiers, and break fallow ground. In the course of their journey to the Promised Land, the Israelites once dwelt on Mt Horeb. But seeing that they were making that location a comfort zone, God admonished them through Moses to move forward (Deuteronomy 1:5-6). That means as a new creation, never be comfortable at the level of prosperity you are at, but rather have a divine drive that lifts you to higher levels and catapults you to the highest realm of abundance.

In the realm of God's prosperity, stagnation, delay or procrastination is abominable, unacceptable and illegitimate. The minute we get born again, we are catapulted onto God's highway and we begin to operate like an emergency vehicle. While other cars are restricted by robots and traffic rules, an emergency vehicle is exempted from all the usual rules.

What it does is to put on a flashing signal and all the cars have to give way or move to the side of the highway; whether robots are red or not, the traffic rules do not apply to the emergency vehicle. By the same token, as we get born again, all the impediments, hindrances and laws of nature responsible for delays due to the limitations of time begin to give way for us to move forward. This is because you have been called to the upward and forward life. While there are those who say that life is full of ups and downs, that shouldn't be your experience of life. You are to journey only in one direction – upward and forward. There is no other option. Your set time for advancement is now. It doesn't matter how things may look around you; if you will let the Spirit guide you, your life will be a story of unending success.

One of the first instructions that God gave Adam was to be fruitful and multiply on the earth. This implies that God's original master plan is for us to increase and advance in life. In Deuteronomy, it speaks of increase of blessings such as divine health, promotion and favour. This law is connected to the law of favour, for it is out of God's favour that increase comes. For example, when Jacob worked for Laban, he began to increase in livestock. Moreover, the Bible proclaims in Acts 19:20 *that in the city of Ephesus so mightily grew the word of God and prevailed.* This implies that in the same way as the word of God spreads, in the realm of prosperity we are also entitled to migrate from tens to hundreds, then from hundreds to thousands and ultimately from thousands to millions and billions in wealth.

35. *The law of divine grace and favour*

This is a spiritual law and principle that supersedes and transcends all laws and principles of the universe. Its connection with the law of prosperity is that prosperity is a by-product of God's grace and sovereignty. According to the law of grace, anyone is entitled to partake in the fullness of God's blessings not because he has done anything impressive but simply because he has been located by grace. In a biblical context, grace is an endowment or impartation which when it is given or granted, produces special abilities in you that reflect on the outside. Grace is supernatural; it is the outward reflection of a divine influence in the human spirit and favour is one of the workings of grace. It is God's favour that qualifies us to experience His glorious benefits in the Kingdom and be catapulted to the realm of millionaires. As a new creation, you have the grace-advantage grace brings acceptability; it's that lifting power of God that attracts the right people, circumstances and resources in line with God's destiny for your life. In the context of the revelation of prosperity, grace is therefore the divine ability in you to be successful in every endeavour; it is the power of promotion and that thing which causes your life to levitate from one level of prosperity to the other. As one who is graced of God, there is a *divine aura* about you that attracts good to you. No wonder Paul proclaimed in Romans 8:28 that *"All things work together for the good."* Even in challenging situations, or in the face of adversity, grace gives you the advantage and causes you to rise above every adversity. Grace differentiates you in this world; it sets you apart for glory and excellence. Therefore in this season, some people will be made millionaires not because they have done anything amazing but just because they have been located by the grace of God. Some will work hard to earn a living and receive a portion of their financial wealth but others will just tap into the realm of God's grace and receive abundance of wealth and financial resources without much effort. This is the prevailing, preeminent principle of God's favour and an extension of God's hand of grace on His creation; hence, no man can question or contend with what God has done under the circumstances. The law of grace brings forth justice and a window of opportunity for the rise of those whom the world has side-lined, prejudiced and oppressed through its corruptive system of governance and deficient financial laws, to a place where they can freely amass Heaven's wealth and financial resources in the capacity of Kingdom millionaires.

God's ever-present desire is to give us all things to enjoy freely, not because of what we have done or who we are, not because we deserve it, but because of who He is, not because we work for it, but because He has always wanted man to enjoy the fullness of His blessings. All the people recorded in the Bible who were very prosperous or rich were not rich because of their own work but by the grace of God. The grace of God supersedes all natural and spiritual laws and it overlaps and touches even those who do not know God. In like manner, every person in this world who is very rich has received their riches by the grace of God, whether they know Him or not, and it is through the law of grace that millions are produced in the Kingdom. You must therefore embrace the reality that the Lord has encompassed you all around with divine favour; hence you can never be disadvantaged, but marvellously helped. You are dressed with divine favour; hence regardless of wherever you are, you can bask in abundance. Therefore never count yourself out or believe that anything is too good for you. If it's the best, then it belongs to you because you are God's best. If only you could come to the consciousness of this reality, doors of blessings and opportunities that cannot be humanly explained will supernaturally be opened for you.

36. *The law of attraction*

There is an intricate divine connection between the law of attraction and amassing huge wealth from God (Exodus 11:3, Deuteronomy 33:23, Joshua 11:20, 1 Samuel 16:22, Esther 2:17, Esther 5:8, Esther 8:5). The law of attraction states that as a recipient of God's anointing, you are a living magnet that perpetually attracts people, situations and circumstances that are in agreement with your dominant thought. The law of attraction therefore states that you can attract anything you want in your life, be it more money, a bigger house, more businesses, a perfect mate, or literally anything you want. The law of attraction is actually a biblical concept expressed in the words of Jesus in Matthew 9:29 when He declared, "*According to your faith, be it unto you,*" and in Mark 9:23 when He proclaimed, "*All things are possible to Him who believes.*" Do you see that He's telling us that there's a connection between our faith and what we attract? This means that if you have faith, then you can attract anything that you want, including millions in wealth. We already saw this truth in the Old Testament verse that states, *as a man thinks, so is he* (Proverbs 23:7). This means that the power of our thoughts can draw or attract to us anything that we want to become. Just by thinking, you already have it; just by believing, you already have it, and, just by seeing it, it is already yours.

The Bible declares in Psalm 23:6, *surely goodness and mercy shall follow me all the days of my life.* This is the law of attraction. The Hebrew word that translates as "follow" means to pursue, attract, chase or run after. This means that millions of God's blessings will chase or run after you. The Bible further records in Deuteronomy 28:2 that *all these blessings shall come upon thee, and overtake thee.* Overtaking is an extreme degree of attraction. At that realm or level, not only are blessings attracted to you but they come in measures that by far exceed your capacity to contain or handle them. It is a fact that some people attract God's blessings while others repel them. Usually, those people who are favoured or anointed will attract God's wealth easily because *money cannot resist the anointing; it always flows in the direction where the anointing is flowing.* The things that determine the law of attraction are the anointing, God's favour, supernatural power and glory and these cannot be resisted by anything in this world. As a matter of fact, all the blessings and financial riches of this world are flowing in the direction in which the anointing, power and glory are flowing. That is why, nowadays, people who operate more in these gifts are the ones who seem to flourish and prosper financially more than others because all the world's resources and Heaven's common wealth are moving or streaming in their direction. This is why it is imperative that you move in the seven dimensions of the supernatural *(faith, anointing, presence, power, mantle, glory and love)* because each has a magnetic force of some kind that attracts money and causes it to flow in its direction.

The law of attraction and God's will can and should work together in your life. The law of attraction is a biblical principle; therefore, it will work for anyone who practises it. I'm sure you've noticed that non-Christian people have achieved great success in their chosen endeavours just as some Christians have. Why? Because they're practising godly principles and they just don't realise it. In the realm of God, there are certain things that you will not have to work hard to claim or loosen; instead, you simply have to attract them. They are automatically magnetised by your presence even without your having to do anything amazing. You simply have to open your spirit wide and they will automatically drop in. This is why it is advisable that, rather than chasing after the substance of money, you should simply get the anointing and money will come; get the favour and the right wife will come; get the power and the right people will flock in your direction.

The law of attraction works through God's favour, for it is favour that attracts or magnetises the blessings of God to a person: promotion, restoration, honour, victory, recognition, preferential treatment and supernatural increase in assets and real estate. Favour is one of the out workings of grace —God's kindness and help extended toward us. It is of paramount importance to emphasise that millions do not come by labour but by favour. God desires that we manifest favour as a lifestyle so that the oil of favour can flow on us every day. Favour is a gift that enables you to succeed where naturally you would have failed. If you have toiled and done everything that you know how but you are not seeing any results, just seek God's favour and things will begin to fall into place. The favour of God is God's personally acting on your behalf, doing for you whatever it takes for you to prosper, thrive, flourish and be the success you were created to be. The favour of God will cause people to go out of their way to bless you, provide for you, help you, assist you and make special concessions just for you. The favour of God will make a way where there is no way, open doors where there are no doors, provide where there is no provision and do the impossible in the midst of the most impossible situations.

37. The law of release

When it comes to matters of Kingdom financial prosperity, the law of release plays a pivotal role in the manifestation of our millions in wealth. The Bible says in Matthew 18:18 *that whatever you shall bind on earth shall be bound in heaven and whatever you shall release in earth shall be released in heaven.* This is the essence of the law of release. It means that if you release millions in wealth, Heaven is bound to act in the direction of your confession. Things are manifest or moved from the realm of the Spirit into the physical realm through release. Unless you release it, it will not manifest. By the same token, you need to step up in faith and release your millions in wealth. It is a spiritual law that if something is not released, it stays bound in the Spirit. This is why God says in Haggai 2:7 *"In just a little while I will again shake the heavens and the earth, the oceans and the dry land."* Why shaking? Because shaking is what releases our blessings that are held by demonic powers in the spirit realm. Did you know that even God has to be released to move on behalf of humanity? To release God means to allow Him, to unreservedly grant Him permission, to move on your behalf. Concerning end-time plans,

God has said that,

The greatest financial inversion of such dimension and magnitude that has ever been witnessed in the history of humanity will break forth and increase abundantly in these days. "Tremendous financial prosperity shall engulf the masses as I unleash the fullness of my desire to move in the realm of your financial prosperity. But release Me," saith the Lord, "release Me that I may come on your behalf and move on your behalf."

Spiritual Laws & Principles of The Kingdom

Regarding the law of release, three locations of our blessings exist. Some of our wealth or blessings are located in the first Heaven, in the Heaven's store house; some of them are located in the spirit realm or dimension in the second Heaven; and some are located here on earth while some are located in you. Therefore, knowing where your blessings are located is a vital step in releasing huge wealth into your life. We can employ or tap into various principles and actions of faith to release these blessings. Those blessings that are located in Heaven are released by placing a demand and appropriating them by faith, those located in the first Heaven and subject to manipulation by principalities are released by command and prophetic declaration, while those located on earth are released by simply possessing them. Those in you are released through activation of gifts and praying in the Holy Ghost. The mistake that many people make is to cry to God for blessings; yet, He has made them readily available for you to access. You can therefore release anything you want, be it money or anything else, and it will come because Heaven works hand in hand with your confession to ensure that whatever you say is released. That is why Jesus is said to be the high priest of our confession because He handles our declarations. Hence, whatever we release is ordained and authenticated in Heaven and He releases it.

38. *The law of action and reaction*

The law of action and reaction states that for every action you take in the supernatural realm, there will always be a corresponding reaction to that action in the natural realm. The Bible proclaims in Luke 6:38: *Give, and it shall be given unto you; good measure, pressed down, and shaken together, and running over, shall men give unto your bosom.* It further says: *ask and it shall be given to you, knock and the door shall be opened.* This implies that there is a response in the Spirit to every action of faith that you take in the natural realm. Giving is a spiritual act and, as you act on it, there is a corresponding response that you receive in the natural realm in the form of blessings. What we do in the Spirit will always elicit a corresponding response in the natural and whatever we do in the natural is always preceded by a corresponding action in the Spirit. The law of action and reaction brings the realm of the natural and realm of the Spirit to work together. Revivals are triggered in this way. God says, *"Ask for me in the time of the latter rain and I will give you showers of rain."* That means that as requests are sent to Heaven, a corresponding response is released to that effect. Moreover, God says *"Call unto me and I will answer thee."* This means that spiritual exercises such as asking and calling are critical in terms of the release of Heaven's huge wealth into our lives.

The Bible makes it clear in Mathew 18:18, that *whatever we bind on earth shall be bound in heaven and whatever we loose on earth shall be loosed in heaven.* This is the basis of the principles of action and reaction.

In other words, as you take a step of faith to loose your blessings, there is a corresponding action that authenticates your loosing from the heavenly realm. On the other side of the coin, as you release your blessings, there is also a corresponding action that validates the release of those blessings from the heavenly realm. Moreover God says in Hebrews 11:6 *"I am a rewarder of those who diligently seek me."* Thus, as you take an action of faith to seek the face of God, God rewards you by unveiling His mysteries to you. It is through this divine principle that you will be able to draw millions of God's blessings in this season.

CHAPTER THREE

SPIRITUAL LAWS OF RESURRECTION & THE RAISING OF THE DEAD

What spiritual principles should we tap into to raise the dead?

It is worth exploring the divine truth that there are laws that God has put in place through which He governs the universe and these are *physical laws* which govern the natural realm and *spiritual laws* which govern the realm of the spirit. For example, there is a *law of gravity* which states that if you throw an object up in the air, it will evidently crash back onto the earth; the *law of floatation* which allows ships and boats to float on water, the *law of aerodynamics* that enables aeroplanes to fly and the *law of electricity* which helps us generate heat and light energy. The reality is that when we operate in obedience to these physical laws within nature, we enjoy them but when we violate them, they hurt us. However, as much as there are physical laws, there are also spiritual laws which are the *highest class of laws* governing and controlling the entire universe. The following are key spiritual laws that we should tap into in order for us to fully operate in the realm of raising the dead:

The Law of Sin and Death

Apostle Frequency Revelator

The law of sin and death implies that death can only operate in humanity where sin is present. In the absence of sin, death is not permitted to reign. For example in heaven there is no sin hence, there is neither death, sickness nor any form of decay. It must be understood right from the onset that the reason behind the alarming deaths of multitudes of people across the world is highly attributable to the root of sin because God said in Ezekiel 18:20 that *a soul that sins shall die*. Death began when Adam sinned and in generations that followed thereafter, the gravity of sin was so intensified to the extent that God regrettably said *My soul shall not strive forever with man, seeing that he is continuously sinning* (Isaiah 59:2; Genesis 6:6). Judgement was then passed on man and the devil took advantage and manipulated the plight of humanity and inflicted man with death traps.

The reality is that the devil has an energy force that he activates in the flesh of unbelievers as a result of the fallen state of man. This is why Paul says in Romans 7: 5, that *when we were in the flesh, the sinful passions which were aroused by the law were at work in our members to bear fruit to death*. This is the energy of the *law of sin and death*. It's like the law of gravity that pulls you down to this earth every time you attempt to rise higher. This energy is activated on the flesh because an unregenerate man is born in sin hence, the law of sin and death is at work. It's the energy that pulls people downwards into sin and death and this is why Paul wrestled with it in Romans 7: 15 where he attests that, *"What I want to do, I don't do but what I don't want to do, that I do it*. In Ephesians 2:2, Paul speaks of the manner in *which we once walked according to the course of this world, according to the prince of the power of the air, the spirit who now works (or energizes) in the sons of disobedience*. The *sons of disobedience* refers to unbelievers. This implies that there is energy of sin that is at work in the lives of unbelievers and if one is tempted by the devil, the energy of sin is so strong that he is drawn like a piece of iron to a magnet. This is the energy of sin, the law of sin and death working in your life.

It must therefore be understood that the battle in our lives as Christians is to know how to harness the energy of our mortal bodies and to crucify the old man or flesh. This is because the flesh provides a fertile ground on which this energy force is activated. However, because God loved what He had created, He had a plan of redemption and sent His only begotten son to die for the sins of all the people. Following the resurrection of Jesus Christ from the dead, the energy of sin and death is disabled, deactivated, mortified and does no longer have any grip of power over us. Hence, we need to always activate the energy force of the Holy Spirit to overcome the energy force of the devil. How do we deactivate the energy or force of sin and death while at the same time activating the law of the spirit of life in Christ? It's through sanctification, righteousness, persuit of holiness, prayer and fasting, meditating on the word of God, and so forth.

The greater truth is that in the absence of sin, death cannot touch a mortal body. Philosophically speaking, death is the presence of sin and the absence of the Holy Spirit in a human body. Jesus was like Adam before he sinned. Adam could be tempted—but before Adam sinned, his body was neither mortal nor immortal. In essence, Adam did not need to sustain that human body by eating. If Adam's body had been mortal, it would have been subject to death—but Adam *originally wasn't subject to death*. The Word of God says that death affects you when you sin: *"Therefore, as by one man sin entered into the world, and death by sin; so death passed upon all men, for that all have sinned"* (Romans 5:12). Death didn't pass on mankind until after Adam had sinned. This is the reason Jesus couldn't be killed until He was made sin for us. Jesus said, *"No man taketh it* [His life] *from me, but I lay it down of myself"* (John 10:18). Once an angry mob was going to throw Him off the brow of a hill at Nazareth to kill Him, but He slipped through their midst and disappeared (Luke 4:29,30). Then, in the Garden of Gethsemane, when He took upon His spirit, our sins and our diseases, His body became mortal, and they could kill Him.

The Law of the Spirit of Life

This is the overarching law which we can tap into in an endeavour to raise the dead. Through this law, we are given the liberty to exercise our rights in the spirit to impart the life of God upon a death victim bring him back to life. The Bible affirms in Romans 8:1-3, that *there is therefore now no condemnation to those who are in Christ Jesus, who do not walk according to the flesh, but according to the Spirit. For the law of the Spirit of life in Christ Jesus has made me free from the law of sin and death.* This implies that the law of the spirit of life is a higher law that sets you free and pulls you out of the clutches of the gravitational pull of sin and death. The solution to the entanglement of the law of sin and death is unveiled in Romans 8:11: *If the Spirit of Him who raised Jesus from the dead dwells in you, He who raised Christ from the dead will also vitalise or give life to your mortal bodies through His Spirit who dwells in you.* This is to show you that the law of sin and death is deactivated by the vitalisation, activation and quickening power of the indwelling Spirit in us.

This implies that there is a different energy that flows in our spirit. As we yield to the Spirit of God, our spirit, soul and body comes under the energy of God. This is why when the Spirit of God comes upon you, it is easy to resist the energy of sin because there is more godly energy than the enemy's energy. To illustrate this revelation with reference to a typological example, there is a certain amount of propulsion for any projectile or spaceship to leave the gravitational pull of the earth. Isaac Newton was the first person to calculate that and to find out how much propulsion is needed to escape the gravitational pull. That is how the spaceships are built big because they need a certain amount or propulsion to escape the gravitational pull. In the same way we need a certain amount of energy force to flow in our lives. If you step out of the energy of the spirit of life, you automatically fall in the realm of the law of sin and death and vice versa.

The Law of righteousness

It must be engraved into our thinking that Jesus was crucified on the cross so that righteousness might prevail upon the world. Righteousness means *being in the right standing with God*. It is an impartation of the nature of God in our spirit, producing in us the ability to do what is right all the time and to stand before God without any fear of condemnation. It is not based on what we have done but on what Jesus has done on the cross. Jesus Christ who knew no sin went to the cross willingly. And that day was a special day for the whole world. It was twelve noon when a righteous and sinless man died a death that He didn't deserve. Do you know that there is a law of God that *all have sinned and come short of the glory of God and the wages of sin is death?* Where there is no sin there must not be any death. Satan in his glee thought he had conquered. All the forces of death rallied against Jesus, and at twelve in the afternoon at the time when the sun was at its peak, the skies were full of dark clouds. Even the planet earth, the weather, the clouds, the mountains, the leaves, the plants, all the kingdom of creation, knew that a righteous innocent man was put to death without one sin in His life. There were tremendous forces at work that day and for a moment when they surrounded Jesus to conquer Him, to put Him to death, in the darkness of separation from God that He took for you and I, Jesus Christ cried out *"Eli, Eli, lama sabachthani?" (My God, My God, why have You forsaken Me?)*. He was left all alone because when sin came, do you know that Jesus died because sin pressed itself upon Him - our sin not His own sin?

Suddenly, it was right at that very moment that righteousness was released. Righteousness came forth. It began as a river from the cross. On the third day, Jesus Christ the righteous, arose and righteousness overcame sin. In the same manner in which good is more powerful than evil, righteousness is also more powerful than sin. As righteousness came forth, it cancelled sin, sicknesses and diseases. It cancelled the handwriting on the wall that was against us, and it cancelled the right of Satan over this world. It cancelled the right of Satan over human kind, and Satan was utterly destroyed. All the principalities were stripped off their powers because righteousness is greater than sin (Colossians 2:15). And on that day the forces of righteousness were imparted and in 2 Corinthians 5:21, it says that *we might become the righteousness of God in Him*. Righteousness is not based on what man has done or not done but on what Jesus has done on the cross at Calvary. Therefore, it is through the law of righteousness that we are elevated into a dimension to command the dead to come back to life and no force of evil can withstand the power of righteousness.

The Law of Love

There is a realm which a man can be catapulted into which marks the highest level of spiritual contact with God. At that level of life, one is not chasing after any needs but rather after the heart of God. It is called the *seventh dimension*. That realm is the realm of love. It is a realm of perfection. It is a dimension in which God Himself lives, breathes and operates. That is a realm in which when catapulted into, man loses his own self-consciousness and begins to think as God thinks, talk as God talks, see as God sees and consequently view all things from God's perspective. In other words, in that realm, man begins to pour out the heart of God into every situation that he encounters. In that realm, everything is complete and perfect. Sickness, pain and death cannot operate in that realm. It is more powerful than any other dimension which man can ever function in this world. Did you know that the most powerful force in the universe is not the force of gravity or magnetic expulsion and repulsion but the energy of Love? When the Bible says that *we have been translated from the Kingdom of darkness into the Kingdom of light*, the word, "*translated*" in its original context in Greek connotes to some aggressive force that comes through love. Love can drag a man from the gravitational pull of hell and catapult him into the highest realm of God. Do you remember that Jesus said, *"If anyone wants to come to me, I will draw him to me"*. In this context, the word, *"Draw"* denotes the gravitation pull or energy of love that attracts, magnetises and lures sinners to the Kingdom of God. Love is therefore a force that can draw millions of souls into the kingdom of light and can also trigger an outbreak of the energy of the anointing through the tidal waves of the air and the torrential flow of the rain of God's power from the *Heaven's power house*, culminating in the greatest miracles ever performed in the history of mankind.

Now, the question is: How is this realm of love related to the raising of the dead? The *resurrection power* is a force of love – only the gravity or force of love can pull a man from the clutches of the worse demons of hell and set his soul free from torments. That is why any man who happens to operate in the realm of love and graduates into perfection, draws the power or divine energy that can cause the dead to jump out of the coffin even without saying a word. It is in this realm that Smith Wigglesworth would drag a dead body from a coffin, thrust it against the wall and then command it to walk. In case you thought love was a subtle, do you now see how aggressive the force of love is? That aggressive force that pulled the dead body from its coffin and commanded it to walk is actually the force of love. The Bible unveils the divine truth that Jesus raised Lazarus from the dead **because He loved him** (John 11:5). In other words, Jesus tapped into the realm of God's love and harnessed the divine energy that magnetised Lazarus's spirit from the spirit world and brought it back into its body. Since Lazarus was saved, it's apparent that his spirit was already in paradise but though the energy of love, Jesus managed to pull it back from Paradise into Lazarus's body in the natural realm. In essence, the bedrock of our Christian faith is the unmerited, fathomless marvel of the love of God exhibited by Jesus Christ on the cross at Calvary, a love men can never and shall never merit. That is why I say love is the most brutal force in the universe because it took love for Jesus to be brutally wounded and butchered on the cross, just to save humanity form sins. Only the force or energy of love can do that.

The greater truth is that the realm of love is a realm of God's glory. It marks the highest level of concentration of God's power. Therefore, if you wish to be mightily used by God in raising the dead as if you are waking people from sleep, it is highly imperative that you don't only operate in the dimension of faith but also in a higher realm of love, which is the *seventh dimension* of the supernatural realm. The Bible enumerates the most critical aspects of divinity which are *faith, hope* but then *love* is said to be the greatest (1 Corinthians 13:13). Why? Because it is a realm in which God Himself operates. God does not need faith or hope to operate but surely He requires love because He is love and love is a foundational pillar in His Kingdom. What actually distinguishes the realm of love from all other realms of God's power is that others can be counterfeited but no one can counterfeit love; it is impossible even for the devil himself to love. That is why the Bible says *if a man can pray in tongues of angles and has the ability to fathom all mysteries but does not have love, he is nothing* (1 Corinthians 1:13). Why? Because the realm of God is the realm of love, hence anybody who wishes to function in the greater depths of the miraculous should have the ingredient of love. God lives in love, He breathes love and speaks the language of love. Therefore, the realm of the miraculous is the realm of love. It is therefore worth mentioning that only those who would manage to tap into the realm of love will be launched into greater depths of raising the dead because this realm is sacred, hence can only be entrusted to those who have stood a test of love.

The Law of action and reaction:

It must be understood that practical demonstration or experimentation is such a vital principle when it comes to the ministry of raising the dead. In other words, it is virtually impossible for the dead to be raised without one taking actions of faith to command the dead to rise up. Death is not automatic. It is either initiated, provoked or set in motion. If there is no corresponding action to validate its manifestation, the dead will not rise up by themselves. If there is no corresponding action of faith that validates, authorises or gives spiritual subjects permission to legally endorse a resurrection, then the dead are not raised. It's as simple as that. You can cry, twirl and twain until your face turns blue but unless you command the dead to arise, they might not be raised. This is because in the realm of the spirit, nothing can be registered as legitimate and acceptable to God if there is no corresponding action effected thereto. Faith without action is as dead as death itself. That is why the Bible concurs in Hebrews 11:6 that *without faith it is impossible to please God.* By the same token, without corresponding action, demonstration or experimentation, it is impossible for the dead to be raised. The only way you can get to know if you have the *resurrection power* is when you demonstrate your actions of faith by praying for the dead.

How will you raise the dead if you never pray for anyone dead to be raised? The dead are not going to vacate the mortuaries and

come into your living room. Instead, you need to be bold enough to go to wherever they are.

The greater truth is that it takes courage and boldness coupled with actions of faith to confront the dead or speak life into a death situation in order to obtain positive results. Jesus is a quintessential example of someone who made practical demonstrations of faith by either touching the casket or speaking directly to the dead to come back to life. According to the law of manifestation, in the realm of the spirit, spiritual subjects are bound to move only when commanded. This is because an action of faith is registered as an input or tangible reality in the realm of the spirit that gives substantial material or license for spiritual subjects to produce whatever results you need. That is why Jesus said *whatever you bind on earth shall be bound in heaven and whatever you release on earth shall be loosed in heaven.* This implies that you need to act on your faith by binding and loosing so that heaven will respond to your actions of faith by releasing a corresponding divine energy to set that which you declare in motion in order to produce the results of what the word talks about. If you don't demonstrate your actions of faith, where do you expect God to get the material needed to magnetise the departed spirit and bring it back into its body? This is because actions of faith are a critical mass and heavy weight substance in the spirit realm that is needed to cause the dead to come back to life. That is why the resurrection power of God will not be precipitated down to earth if there are no corresponding actions of faith to validate or authenticate its release.

But what exactly constitutes the actions of faith? Actions can be expressed in two different ways; it's either they come in the form of *words* or *demonstrations*. Do you know that everything that is created, whether living or dead has sound waves, a rhythm embedded in it and a voice that hears and obeys when commanded to. By the same token, even a dead corpse has a sound waves and a rhythm that responds when you command it to come back to life. It might not have an active mouth to express itself anymore but it has a rhythm that hears. Do you remember that Jesus spoke to a fig tree such that it listened and obeyed the results of which it instantly withered? If a fig tree, an inanimate object, worse than a dead corpse could hear the voice of Jesus, obey and wither instantly, how much more would we not speak to the dead body and command it to come back to life. Even though it might not be showing any signs of movement in the natural realm, in the realm of the spirit, it surely has a rhythm that responds when commanded to. Armed with this revelation, it makes you realise that your mission to raise the dead is as easy as taking a stroll through a park.

The Law of divine purpose

Divine Purpose is such a vital determining factor or pulling force when it comes to matters of raising the dead. The dead are not just raised for fun or for popularity purposes but for a specific purpose. Every act of resurrection is connected to a specific divine purpose. Without purpose the dead are not raised. The purpose of resurrection could be to ascribe unto God all glory, honour and power due His Name, to usher an unprecedented avalanche of billions of souls into the Kingdom, or to liberate humanity from the bondage of the devil. Resurrection in itself is not an end but a means to an end; the end is that humanity might come to know Christ, receive Him and fulfil the original purpose for which they were brought into this world. Concerning Pharaoh, God said,

> *"For this purpose have I raised you, to show my power, that my name may be glorified"* (Exodus 9:16).

In other words, although Pharaoh was a cruel man, his cruelty could not rule out the fact that God had raised Him for a particular purpose. Does it amaze you that God raised Pharaoh to be cruel to the Israelites? The greater truth is that purpose is one greater spiritual law and principle that overrules other laws. Because of God's purpose, other laws are frozen or held constant so that His will and purpose could prevail. To substantiate this veiw with reference to further scriptural evidence, when Jesus was crucified, He said it was for a purpose that He be crucified otherwise if not, He would have called His Father to send more than twelve legions or battalions of angels to rescue him (Mathew 26:53). The same applies with raising people from the dead. In this special and sacred ministry, purpose prevails more than anything else. As a result, some people whom the world never thought could be raised from the dead will be surely raised for the sake of fulfilling God's purpose.

The Law of grace

It must be entirely registered in people's minds that the law of grace is an overarching law that rules over all the laws of the universe. This is because grace is administered directly by God Himself through His sovereignty and mercy as the sole owner of the universe. Therefore, every resurrection is undertaken within the context of God's grace. It is by grace that the dead are raised and not by our own wishes and desires. Contrary to what multitudes of believers presume, is not because we have great faith that we are able to raise the dead although faith has a greater part to play in the resurrection. Even faith itself gets to a level where it falters when the law of grace is introduced. Faith works in the absence of grace but when grace shows up, faith disappears. Even Faith itself operates within the frame work of the law of grace. That is why through grace, God raises the people whom the world does not approve, recognise or honour in any way and uses them to raise the dead for His glory. By grace, God chooses whom He wants to use in this special and sacred ministry regardless of race, age, level of education and other disparities of humanity.

Smith Wigglesworth, a man who raised a large number of people from the dead than anybody else in the world is said not to have had any formal education, yet he operated in higher realms and dimensions of resurrection. Apparently, he never attended any school or training session except Bible classes, where he was actually taught by his own wife how to read the Bible, yet he moved in such greater depths and higher dimensions of resurrection than the most powerful man on earth right now. The only explanation is GRACE. Therefore, one must never be tempted to think that now that we have been ushered into a season of global resurrection revival, God is going to use the most prominent preachers for such a purpose. This is because God's ways are not our ways (Isaiah 55:8). You will be shocked to find God using some men in backyard ministries who are not even known in their own streets. This is called *election by grace*. Remember that in election, God does not look at the outward appearance and He demonstrated this principle very well by the way He chose or selected David a shepherd boy to be King over Israel, instead of the tall and handsome Saul.

CHAPTER FOUR

SPIRITUAL LAWS AND PRINCIPLES OF OPERATING IN THE REALM OF ANOINTING

There are three main keys to operating in the anointing. The first key is to discern the purpose and type of anointing manifesting. The third key is to receive the manifestation of the anointing. The second is to learn how to channel the manifested anointing. However, there are other divergent keys that we can use to unlock the supernatural realm and release the rain of the anointing in a greater measure. Any man of God who seem to be moving in deeper dimensions of the anointing is because he has learnt the art of tapping into these principles. There is a difference between being anointed and being able to propagate the anointing. Some man of God are anointed by their anointing is not seen because they have not learnt the principles of how to channel it, direct it and cause it to rain upon the masses. The following are therefore keys that can unlock the treasure of the anointing in your spirit and catapult you to greater dimensions of the anointing you have never dreamed possible.

46. *The Law of Releasing the anointing*

A lot of believers have the believer's anointing but they don't know how to release it. The only way to keep the anointing is to give it away. The anointing can be released through *faith* and *confession*. Therefore, one of the key laws of operating in the believer's anointing is to understand the power of words. Words are the capsules that contain the believer's anointing and release it forth. The believer's anointing in all fve realms depends on the word we speak. The next time you want to release the believer's anointing over anything, speak it out verbally. That is why we say grace over food. You know we are releasing tremendous authority and power over substances that you partake of. When you make a confession over your home, you are releasing the anointing, and this anointing is not the anointing upon but the anointing within. Words are powerful and believers are not using them enough. You are not taking authority. *Exousia* is not operating. Believers are just as dumb as Adam standing next to the woman letting her talk to the serpent. David was a man of war. However, we see that his life was marked with a tremendous outflow of worship and psalms. Remember, we said that where there is an *inflow* there is an *outflow*. Unless we release the outflow, there is no further inflow of the anointing into our life. Whenever the anointing comes upon David's life, he would always sing or speak forth God's praises in songs and psalms. This is the essence of releasing the anointing. He expressed himself in worship unto God. There is an outflow from his life. There could be many types of outflow in different lives or even in the same life, there could be many types of outflow but some outflows would feature more prominently than others. In David's life, the outflow of the psalms and worship stands out strongly. He is known as a sweet psalmist of Israel. In other people's lives, the outflow may be strongly manifested in other areas. In some people's lives, the outflow is shaking. They may not be that good in singing and worshiping. That is not their field. When the anointing comes into their life, they get into a shaking. I am not saying that the Holy Spirit causes all types of manifestations. There could be demonic imitation or it could be just simply the flesh. However, that does not rule out the fact that there are genuine ones. The problem is not whether there is a manifestation or not. It is a matter of discerning the type and origin of the manifestations. A manifestation of shaking comes on some people. For some people, the anointing is manifested through prophesying. Some people would just rock to and fro when the anointing of God comes upon their life. When the tangible anointing of God in a person's life is released, demons can sense it very much because they are creatures in the spirit world. Demons know what spiritual substance is. Human being tends to live more on the flesh and be more conscious of the flesh area. Demons are very sensitive to the spirit world because they themselves are spirit beings. So when you take the anointing and put on some person who is attacked by demon, the demon feels it even more that that person.

Some people only moved into level one. At level one, we learn to recognize how it comes. At level two, we learn when it is not there how to bring it about. We need to know how to discover your particular way of bringing down the anointing. How do we discover the way in which the anointing can come in our life? By examining your particular manifestation when you frst receive the anointing. When you first received the anointing and you prophesy you can be assured that you keep on prophesying to maintain it. If the anointing came upon you and your hand shakes, the next time you want the anointing of God, wait on Him, get into the atmosphere you learn and you stir and you sense that little handshake coming. Now, this kind of stirring is a little bit like Samson. Let us look at Samson as he operates in the anointing. In the book of Judges, Samson has a particular way of moving in the anointing and his anointing was tremendous. He had such a powerful strength that came supernaturally. I want to point to you the fact that when his head was shaved and his covenant was broken, the anointing was lifted up from him. In Judges 16, a phrase there gives you an incident that could point to how he did it in verse 20. And she said, *"The Philistines are upon you, Samson!"* Therefore, he awoke from his sleep, and said, *"I will go out as before, at other times, and shake myself free!"* But he did not know that the Lord had departed from him. When Samson had the anointing come upon his life, he seems to have this shaking. When he wants the anointing, he seems to get it. Let me point to some local kind of situation that you could identify it with. There is a sense where you know that the anointing is bubbling forth you just have to release it for it to come forth. In any meeting or in any situation where you know that the anointing is hovering and ready to be released, you know exactly when it will be released. You could sense it. You could withhold it also. On the other hand, you could release more of it when you learn how the anointing comes on your life and what its side effects are.

What other ways could it be experienced? Some people may not experience that kind of warmth. They may experience it differently. They may experience a kind of cold wind blowing. It does not mean that it always has to be hot. Some people say that since God is hot, then cold sensation is from the devil. Hell is hot too. We cannot use that as a theology. For whatever reason sometimes when people sense the anointing they feel this cold shower over them. It comes in waves. Therefore, they have to learn to recognize when it comes, how it comes. If you observe Kathryn Kuhlman very carefully, she always lifts up her hands. Some people would need to lift up their hands before they get it. For example, in your first experience, you sensed the bubbling of the anointing of God and found that the anointing was released when you just lifted up your hands. Then the next time you sense the bubbling, you release it by lifting up your hands again, and the same anointing comes. Your particular anointing is released through what I call a release of faith God has given to you. It is just as if God has given you a teaching anointing you would have the confidence to operate in it even though at that time you are invited you don't have the anointing upon you. Let's say suddenly you are called to teach. You could depend on that teaching anointing to bring forth the Word through your life. You could allow it to have demands made on the anointing of God. You developed a confidence in the grace and the gift of God in your life.

In this level two is that not only do we learn how to stir it, the way we learn to stir it is to recognize the peculiarity of how it first outflow through our life. When the first outflow of the anointing happened when you praised and worshipped God, or when you lifted up your hands, or playing your guitar, maintain what you did. Remember in all these outward manifestations, it is assumed that your relationship with God is fine. If your relationship with God is not fine, you will be like Samson, thinking that since you have been moving in the anointing regularly by a particular release of faith, it will come automatically. However, if you have left the Holy Spirit, and you tried to release the anointing by your usual release of faith, nothing will happen. When you know there is a peculiar way in which it always comes, you could rely on it as long as your relationship with the Holy Spirit is right. You could rely on it as surely as you rely on a weapon in your life, which you have learned to use. You could definitely rely on that when you learned to operate in that and you know the anointing is on that. When your relationship is not right and you try to rely on that, you will be like Samson. You go through all the motions, the right actions, but if you have no relationship with the Holy Spirit, nothing comes forth but the flesh. It works if you have a relationship with the Holy Spirit but it does not work if you do not have a relationship with the Holy Spirit. It wasn't just the mantle—the hairy coat—that divided the waters; if it had been, everyone could have parted waters, because they all wore skin coats—*it was the anointing that did it*. That's why the sons of the prophets said, *"The spirit of Elijah does rest on Elisha."*

In this very hour in which we are living, the Lord is releasing His anointing on His people to a degree unseen since the first century. He wants to not only anoint us, but He wants to teach us how to steward it, how to release it, and how to increase it in our lives. He wants to give us spiritual victory. It is critically important that we be alert and ready to step into this season of divine appointment. God is calling us to welcome His anointing and take our places in the most glorious hour of the Church. God is imparting His anointing to us for our own healing and deliverance, but there is more. He wants us to be so empowered and energized with His anointing that we become instruments of His miracles for others. It is the anointing that breaks the yoke. We are coming into a new prophetic hour, and God is calling us to become carriers of His glory that will break the yokes of bondage, sin and sickness and set His people free wherever we go. A key to walking in and releasing the anointing is love. Everything Jesus did was motivated by His compassion: *"But when He saw the multitudes, He was moved with compassion for them"* (Matthew 9:36). In the same way, anyone who carries the healing anointing must also carry a heart consumed with compassion for those in need. The spirits of pride, criticism, condemnation, prejudice, legalism and judgmentalism are completely incompatible with the anointing of the Spirit. In order to do the works of Jesus, we must be *like* Jesus. The only way to be like Jesus is to let Him live His resurrection life in us.

47. The Law of Recognition or acknowledgement of the anointing

There is an anointing on you, whether you recognize it or not, if you're called to any office or ministry. No matter which office you stand in, or what you are called to do, you can have something to do with determining the *degree of* your anointing. You can prepare yourself for this anointing. If it doesn't come on you, it's because you didn't prepare yourself. Therefore, we all must recognize the anointing coming in our life. You must know when it comes. Recognize the sensation; recognize the tangibility, and how it comes to your life. God is not against us analysing this thing. Therefore, we need to recognize how it comes into our life. If every time the anointing comes upon you and your hands feel like shaking, you know the anointing is there for you. There is another sub-law that we bring into this. Our experience of the Lord can change as we grow in the Lord. You must add in that factor. Once we learn to recognize His manifestation and how it comes, be aware of this sub-point, as we grow in Him and walk with Him through the years, His manifestation in our life can change. In other words, He may not exactly manifest the anointing like He did to you two or three years ago. You will know the change as it comes. Usually the change comes at each phase.

There are different phases in the graduation of the anointing. Usually when we move from one phase to the next phase, the sensation changes. You experience changes in the anointing upon your life when you enter a new phase in your life and ministry. You know that it is a different phase and a different anointing of God that you are moving in. We keep growing from glory to glory, phase to phase in a different anointing of God. You must not forget this sub-clause. Otherwise, you may keep looking for the old manifestation and familiar anointing when God is bringing you to a new phase and new working in your life. Why is it that way? There are so many varied manifestations of the anointing, each of them having a different effect on our life. If you understand the peculiarities and the specific tangibility of the anointing in your life and you know that it's God not the flesh, do not try to do it when you are still in the flesh and no anointing has descended upon you yet. When you know that is God, then you release yourself into them. It becomes your way of knowing when the anointing has come.

48. The Law of Perceiving the anointing or discerning the anointing

To have a manifestation of the anointing is to tangibly perceive the anointing. We need to perceive the anointing, when it is there and when it is not, then a lot of spiritual progress is going to be made by the Church. Like Elisha, unless we know the Spirit has come upon us, we could not operate our spiritual offices (2 Kings 3). The tangibility of the anointing can be sensed in different ways by different individuals. There are varieties of operations (1 Corinthians 12:6). Whatever the method or way of sensing, we must discern the manifestation when it comes. If we are not able to receive the first key of having the anointing manifested in our lives, we should spend our time meditating on the Word of God (*not just reading*), worshipping God in tongues and with the understanding, and praying many hours in tongues. Praying in tongues energizes us to a level where we can easily sense the anointing. Once we have a manifestation of the anointing we can familiarize ourselves with it, making it easier and easier to sense the anointing. It would also take a shorter time to receive the anointing from thenceforth.

Therefore, it is imperative to discern the purpose or type of anointing manifesting. There are many types of anointing and each produces a different work. The healing anointing cannot be used for teaching and vice versa. The anointing to get people baptized in the Spirit cannot be used for healing. There are as many anointings as there are of the types of work of the Holy Spirit. Some types of anointing manifest the side effect of falling under the power. However, in the teaching anointing (*the Spirit of wisdom and revelation*), there is no sense in people falling because they need to consciously hear and understand as well as refer to their Bibles. When manifesting the anointing to get people baptized with the Holy Spirit, it is more important to have them speak with tongues than to have them fall under the power. It is alright if they fall and speak in tongues at the same time but many times I have observed that those ministering are satisfied when they fall, without helping them into the realm of tongues. The sign of receiving the baptism in the Holy Spirit is speaking in tongues and not falling under the power.

Other people might perceive the anointing only through a warm sensation in my heart. I felt like Luke 24 when Jesus was walking with the two disciples on the way to Emmaus. After Jesus disappeared and when they realized it was Jesus, they said to one another, "*Did not our hearts warm when He spoke?*" I felt that sensation. After that, the anointing began to operate a little bit differently, where I not only sense warmth over my heart area, I sensed a warmth all over my head. Therefore, it increased. Together with that, I get a few other peculiar signals for different types of sicknesses, diseases, and problems. I learn to recognize the peculiarity of these manifestations. I moved into that for some time. Later on, the Lord changed it again and now I feel warmth from the top of my head to the tip of my toes. When the anointing for revelation comes, I sense it flow at the centre of my head. When the prophetic anointing comes upon me, I feel it as a sensation in my heart area and when the anointing for signs and wonders comes, my right hand shakes vehemently. For Kenneth Hagin, the anointing is like a coat thrown over him. Each person has a peculiar way of experiencing it. However, peculiar and particular you must learn to recognize the anointing of God in your life. How does it come and what does it do? That is the first area, recognize your individual peculiarity of your anointing and once you have mastered that, tapping into greater dimensions of the anointing for signs and wonders will be like a stroll through a park.

49. *The Law of Activating the anointing*

Smith Wigglesworth once said in his book. " When the Holy Ghost does not move, I move the Holy Ghost". That is a very strange statement to say. When you take that statement out of context, it can give rise to dangerous ideas. The Holy Spirit is God, and we cannot arm-twist Him to do our bidding. However, Smith Wigglesworth is saying that he has learned to recognize how the Holy Spirit moves. He knows like Elisha how to get into the anointing when he has a need. He knows how to move into the anointing when he needs it. That is where we say we need to understand our own peculiar sensation and know how to stir the anointing. Therefore, one of the most valuable lessons to learn in Christ is to stir it up inside of you. Each of us are anointed differently. One thing is clear it is the anointing (*or the empowerment of the Holy Spirit*) that defeats the enemy (Isaiah 10:27): *And it shall come to pass in that day, that his burden shall be taken away from off thy shoulder, and his yoke from off thy neck and the yoke shall be destroyed because of the anointing.* A yoke is a heavy band tied upon the shoulders typically binding two oxen together to force them to use their strength to labour for that person guiding them.

The anointing upon does not remain permanently on our life. When the work is over that it has come to perform the anointing is lifted off. There are times where there is a demand made on the anointing and when it is not there we need to learn to stir it forth. Elisha had firstly learned to recognize his individual peculiarity of his anointing and secondly, he also learned how to get the anointing when it was not there. He learned how to stir up what was called to be upon his life and what was rightfully his to function in. He learned to stir it up. He purposely asked for a musician. While the musician played, it must have helped him to get into a certain stage where he could move into the anointing of God. David was a psalmist. In the anointing upon, (*we are not talking about the anointing within*) the anointing upon comes and goes as the Spirit wills. The anointing upon does not remain permanently on our life. When the work is over that it has come to perform, the anointing is lifted off. There are times where there is a demand made on the anointing and when it is not there we need to learn to stir it forth. Elisha learnt how to stir it up and likewise, David learnt the same. Suppose David wanted to draw on a greater measure of the anointing, I know the first thing that he would do. He would take his harp and play it until the anointing comes upon him. Music plays a big role in the anointing upon. If you watch Kathryn Kuhlman's videotapes, you will find that music played a big role in her moving into the anointing upon her life. Kenneth E. Hagin has also mentioned that. You could be ministering under the anointing upon but if suddenly the musicians play the wrong music, the Holy Spirit is grieved and the anointing is lifted up. There is an anointing upon that we learn to recognize. David learnt to get it by music. Notice he says in one of his psalms that songs of deliverance encompass him.

Spiritual Laws & Principles of The Kingdom

It is recorded in I Samuel 10:5 that, *after that you shall come to the hill of God where the Philistine garrison is. And it will happen, when you have come there to the city, that you will meet a group of prophets coming down from the high place with a stringed instrument, a tambourine, a fute, and a harp before them and they will be prophesying.* Notice the word there *"they will be prophesying."* Now this is a group of prophets. They were stirring the anointing upon their life through music. The anointing was definitely upon them. As Saul passed by, the anointing that was upon their life jumped off them and came on Saul. There was an anointing upon. The question is why they were doing what they were doing. Why won't this group of prophets sit cross-legged under the terebinth tree waiting on God? It was not their way to stir up the anointing of God. The way that they had discovered for their lives was to constantly play music. It stirs the anointing on their life. They had reached level two.

See, in the book of 2 Kings Chapter 3, Elisha was asked to prophesy because the three kings had problems and Elisha said in verse 13 Then Elisha said to the king of Israel, *"What have I to do with you? Go to the prophets of your father and the prophets of your mother."* But the king of Israel said to him, *"No, for the Lord has called these three kings together to deliver them into the hand of Moab."* And Elisha said, *"As the Lord of hosts lives, before whom I stand, surely were it not that I regard the presence of Jehoshaphat king of Judah, I would not look at you, nor see you. But bring me a musician."* Then it happened, *when the musician played, that the hand of the Lord came upon him. And he said thus says the Lord.* See, he recognized the anointing coming on him. Before that, he recognized that it was not there. I can observe that Elisha knew what the anointing was like in his own life. He knew it when it came. He knew it when it was not there. He must have some way of knowing. Therefore, he has reached that first point where he learnt to recognize the peculiarity of his own anointing. That takes experimentation. These things that we teach you got to put into practice the next time that you move into the anointing. Sometimes when you start and you are not sure but you examine it after everything is over to see how the anointing was. To see whether there was really an anointing, check the result. See the anointing produces results.

50. *The Law of Channelling the anointing*

Once we have discerned the type of anointing, we have to discern how to channel it. Channelling the anointing means directing it or flowing in the direction in which the Holy Spirit wants the anointing to move. Whenever the anointing comes upon a place, it fills the atmosphere but we must know how to place a demand or make a pulling on that mantle so that we can move in a specific direction to give birth to supernatural manifestations in the natural realm. For example, if a healing anointing is present, we would have to listen carefully to the Holy Spirit whether He wants us to lay hands on them, use oil, have them lay hands on themselves, have them stand in a row and blow on them or use handkerchiefs. There are always many, many ways to channel the same anointing. Channelling is a release of faith and anointing at the same time. Notice that Jesus uses a variety of methods to channel the healing anointing: by the spoken word, by using clay, by spitting or by touch. Jesus was sensitive to the Holy Spirit and did not patent a method. Many preachers are not sensitive to the Holy Spirit on this third key. They are satisfied with the first two and get stereotyped on one method for channelling the anointing. The methods of channelling the anointing are determined by the specific instructions of the Holy Spirit on each occasion, by the level of anointing manifesting and by God's personal instruction to the minister to operate a method. God sometimes requires certain individuals to use a particular method e.g. Moses using the rod – Exodus 4:17, believers laying hands – Mark 16:18, elders anointing with oil – James 5:14). The best approach in this third key is to keep an open ear to the Holy Spirit even when we have discerned the manifested anointing.

Why does the demon come out when handkerchiefs were laid on the sick? They must have felt something. They did not hear any command. They did not hear any voice. Whether they were hanging inside or outside the person's soul or body, the moment the handkerchief came and touched that person, the demons would feel the force that pushes them away. Some thing would expel them. There was some force that prevents them from hanging on to that body. It was the anointing of God being channelled for a purpose and for a reason. The anointing of God can be channelled. In other words when the anointing is there, you can just leave it there and nothing will happen. You need to take the anointing of God and channel it. Electricity was in the air ever since this world was made. But it has only been in the 20th century that man has been able to tap on the power of electricity that was in the air all along. As long as the anointing of God is in the air, we can draw it in and channel it to perform a task. We can channel it to perform deliverance. We can channel it to do anything. And it is a tangible force that is there. That is the anointing of God. A tangible force was there. When the woman with the issue of blood touched Jesus, Jesus felt something flowing out. No word was spoken or anything. In fact Jesus was on the way to Jairus' house. There was a release at that point and the anointing goes. So there is a point of release. When you reach a person before the point of release there wouldn't be any flow of the anointing of God.

The level of anointing manifested determines the methods of channelling to be used. At a low level of manifested anointing, Jesus used the method of laying on of hands (Mark 6:5). At the beginning of His ministry, Jesus laid hands on everybody in a house meeting (Luke 4:40). Later in His ministry, as His fame increased and expectations and faith of the people grew, Jesus did not have to even lay hands (Mark 6:56; Matthew 14:36). Jesus' methods were determined by the faith level of people. For those who had the faith to receive without the need for laying on of hands, Jesus ministered accordingly (Matthew 8:8). It is interesting to note that Jesus had intended to personally minister when He said, *"I will come and heal him"* (Matthew 8:7). However, since the centurion's faith level was such that a spoken word would suffice, He ministered accordingly. We should therefore not be restricted to a stereotype method of ministering but we should flow with the level of anointing manifested. So when the strength of the anointing comes, then you can do many things with it. You must be careful that when you channel your anointing, your consciousness must be to impart a blessing. Not just for the phenomena but a tangible blessing. So it is a tangible force of anointing. And for that very reason different preachers have different styles. Whatever styles you have, you must watch that you do not just play games. But when you do play games you will not progress to the level of mighty miracles. I am talking about something very serious here. A lot of the people of God today are playing all these kinds of phenomena.

51. Practising the anointing:

In the realm of the anointing, there is another dimension called *practising the anointing*. The anointing requires practice. In the natural, it is the same way. If you expect to be very good at music, you have to discipline yourself to sit down at those instruments and play it and practice. In the natural, practice makes perfect. In the spiritual, you also need practice to make the gifts of God perfect. You just have to practice it until you are accurate in your flow of the anointing of God. Faithfulness is a tremendous key to grow into the next level of the anointing that God has on our life. This helps us to move into a different phase of ministry that He has for our life. We have to be faithful in those areas. Just be faithful to fellowship with the Holy Spirit; get more Word into you; just be faithful to spend more time in praise and worship; just be faithful to spend more time in prayer. When you spend a lot of time before the face of God, you will build your spiritual voltage to the level where you could sense the tangibility of the anointing. We touch a point to cover those who do not seem to feel any manifestation of the anointing. When you reached a stage where you have a tangibility that is where we must recognize its tangibility and manifestation, pinpoint it, and understand what it is telling you. Then check yourself how it felt; what was it like; how did it come -it takes a lot of experimentations. These things that we learn you need to keep practicing them until it becomes a part of you. After several times you learn to recognize it. Learn to recognize its peculiar sensation in your life.

52. The Law of Accommodating the anointing

In order to experience a greater manifestation of the anointing in your life, you need to create space and room for the anointing. Accommodating the anointing is an act of creating a conducive spiritual atmosphere and climate for the rain of the anointing to thrive, operate and precipitate over the masses. It means creating a viable platform and opportunity for the anointing to be manifested tangibly and visibly in the natural realm. In 1 Kings 4, the Shunamite woman created room for Elijah and by so doing it enabled Elijah to operate in miracles, signs and wonders even unto healing her son. When restricted or uninvited, the anointing might not work fully. That is why the bible says *whoever receives a prophetic received the prophetic reward. What is the prophetic reward?* It is the prophetic anointing. It can only operate when received, accommodated and a space created wide enough to allow the anointing to operate. Accommodating the anointing infers developing your capacity to contain the anointing. Some people's spirits are so underdeveloped such that even if the anointing comes in abundance, they are not capacitated to receive it. That is why Jude says in Jude 20 that *builds up your most Holy faith by praying in the Holy Ghost.* Praying in the Holy Ghost is one of the ways of enlarging your spiritual capacity so that you can contain the anointing. It is a pity that multitudes are not able to move in the anointing because they have not created enough space or room to contain the anointing. The greater truth is that the glory of God is immensely revealed where He is welcome. At times believers are so preoccupied with their empty church programmes and agendas such that they hardly create room for a deeper manifestation of the anointing. That should never be your portion.

53. The Law of Maintaining the anointing

There is such a key factor in the realm of the anointing called *maintaining the anointing*. Many ministers of God do not know how to maintain the anointing

Spiritual Laws & Principles of The Kingdom

after they have received it. They would operate in the anointing for some time and then fizzle out. It is one thing to receive an anointing; yet it is another to maintain and increase it. The key to maintaining the anointing is a fasted life. The Lord wants to fll us with His power. He wants us to walk in His anointing so that He can pour out His love, His blessings, His compassion and His healing mercy over the world. For most Christians, receiving the anointing is not the problem; the challenge is *keeping* it. We receive the anointing when we come to Jesus in faith and repentance. The Holy Spirit comes to us and takes up permanent residence in our heart. As we learn to listen to and obey His voice, and as we are filled with the Spirit, we begin to see more and more of the evidence of the presence and increase of the anointing in our lives. This is not easy to keep it because it requires that we die to self. Only the smell of our burning flesh on the altars of our selfishness will release the full fragrance and potency of the anointing. We can't keep the anointing by hoarding it for ourselves. The only way to *keep* the anointing is to give it away. Keeping the anointing means learning to focus on the primary things. First of all, we need to focus on Jesus Christ. He is our Saviour, our Lord and our all in all. Focusing on Jesus means getting to know Him better and better and growing to love Him more and more.

Ministers must learn to walk in the anointing daily. We cannot expect that because we knew an anointing in God a few months or years back that we are automatically walking in the anointing now. It is true that the anointing abides, but we also must abide in the anointing! A "has-been" will not accomplish anything for God unless he first gets back into the flow of the anointing. We can all examine our own hearts in this area and need to continually so that nothing creeps in unawares and robs us of the fulfilment of the Holy Spirit in our lives. Remember Samson (Judges Chapters 13 to 16)? He knew the power of God's Spirit in a mighty way, but he drifted away to the point that he did not even know when the Spirit of God had departed from him! He did not recognize or discern the change taking place; he just "took it for granted" that God was still with him, but He wasn't. We must guard against the same apathy in our own hearts.

Secondly, we need to cultivate a personal relationship with the Holy Spirit. Get to know Him, welcome Him and drink daily and deeply of His water of life. The Holy Spirit is a Person. He is coexistent, coeternal and coequal with God. He is our Helper, Teacher, and Comforter. He is the Resident Lord of the Church. He gives spiritual gifts to empower and anoint you to reflect our glorious Bridegroom Jesus. He transforms us from glory to glory. One of the surest ways to diminish the power of the anointing in your life is to neglect your personal relationship with the Holy Spirit. We can grieve Him with our stubbornness, by gossip, by backbiting other Christians or by other misdirected words, actions or attitudes of the heart. Staying in tune with the Holy Spirit requires daily repentance –allowing the Holy Spirit to expose our thoughts and attitudes in His perfect light and turning to Him and His grace to transform us more and more into Christ's image.

The anointing is maintained by fasting and prayer. Fasting alone does not do much but fasting combined with prayer, or fasting combined with faith, releases tremendous spiritual resources. In modern civilizations, fasting is the act of releasing our consecration and expectation in God. Many tribal people would sometimes travel for days and weeks to reach an evangelistic or healing service. Their 'act' of walking and travelling is a release of their faith and expectation. In modern cities today, we travel to meetings by air-conditioned transportation and reach a meeting with less sacrifice than the tribal people. In tribal places, people come along when they are really keen or have high expectations (it would take high expectations to be willing to travel for days and weeks through the jungles) whereas in modern cities, people casually 'drop by' just to see what is going on. When the disciples asked Jesus why they could not cast out the demon, Jesus pointed to their unbelief (Matthew 17:20). His recommendation was that they fast and pray (Matthew 17:21). The disciples had received the power and authority to cast out demons. They had the ability. They had the anointing. Jesus knew that the anointing had waned in His disciples' lives and thus instructed them to fast and pray. Fasting and prayer are keys to maintaining the anointing of God in our lives. Fasting does not change God but it will definitely change us. Our spiritual hunger, visions and desires are intensified in a fast.

54. *The Law of Walking in the anointing*

It is imperative that we desire more than anything to continuously walk in the anointing. One thing I have learned is that receiving an anointing is very easy because in some cases people just receive it as an impartation from a man of God. However, in order to walk in the anointing, there is a price to pay, and it is a heavy price. To receive the anointing and to walk in it are two entirely different things. It must be understood that we neither run nor fy in the anointing but we walk in the anointing. Walking in the anointing implies taking practical steps to graduate from one level of the anointing to the other. Remember that the anointing is the second dimension of the supernatural realm. Therefore, in order for you to operate mightily in that realm, you must be first catapulted

Spiritual Laws & Principles of The Kingdom

from faith (*first dimension*), through the second dimension to the third dimension.

55. The Law of Timing in the anointing

The next point that we have to understand is to know to be faithful to the timing for each level of anointing. Timing in the anointing implies having the ability to accurately project the next level of operation in the anointing. It involves accurately discerning when a greater measure of the anointing has been released for one to move to the next level and what to do when one gets to the new level. In the same way the sons of Issachar had an acute understanding of the times and seasons and new exactly what Israel ought to do, at a time, you can be catapulted to the realm of prophetic perception to accurately discern the timing of various phases of the anointing in your life.

Timing in the anointing involves operating in the right anointing, at the right time, in the right season at the right place and to the right (people) congregation.

In the case of David, the lion and bear were the testing but this one is different. It's the timing. Do you know that David had the power to conquer Israel during his seven years? He could have defeated them. He had an army that was stronger than the Israelites. The only reason he didn't do that was because he knew God didn't want him to do it. He waited and abided his time. Timing is important. When the people came it was the timing of God. He was anointed three times. First time by Samuel, second time by the tribe of Judah and third time by all of Israel.   *David had three anointing*   . And each time he moved into a different phase of ministry

CHAPTER FIVE

SPIRITUAL LAWS AND PRINCIPLES THAT PROVOKE MIRACLE MONEY INTO MANIFESTATION IN THE NATURAL REALM

What Key Principles Do I Need To Unlock The Grace of Miracle Money?

Most Christians believe that God does release Miracle money, but simply believing that God is able to do it is not enough. You must know the parameters and principles of how to receive it, manifest or demonstrate it in the natural realm. There are key spiritual laws that you can tap into in order to release Miracle money. There are certain principles that one can tap into in order to walk into the deeper realities of God's power in the arena of supernatural financial provision. Just like there are laws of gravity which governs how to operate in the natural realm, there are also spiritual laws that govern the spirit realm or how to operate in the realm of the miraculous. These laws of the supernatural complement each other and are progressions to enter into the greater depths of God. Each of these laws has a specific manifestation that produces something special. These should be applied correctly in order to produce the results of what the Word of

God talks about. If you correctly apply these principles, you will provoke an unprecedented flow of Miracle money in your life and ministry than ever before. However, it is unfortunate that many believers are failing to operate in the realm of the miraculous because they do not understand spiritual laws and principles which they could take advantage of to generate positive results. Spiritual laws and principles are therefore vital keys that unlock the doors into the supernatural and accentuate an avenue through which the power of God can flow.

THE SEVEN-FOLD DIVINE PRINCIPLES OF THE GLORY REALM WHICH CAN PROVOKE THE RAIN OF MIRACLE MONEY INTO MANIFESTATION IN THE NATURAL REALM

56. THE LAW OF PROPHETIC DECLARATION

In the glory realm, things happen the instant they are declared.

There is a new prophetic dimension in the glory whereby things are coming to pass as they are being said. In the glory realm, there is no procrastination, or delays because time is inconsequential. It is for this reason that Miracle money appears in the physical realm the instant it is commended to. When God declared in an atmosphere of glory, *let there be light*, light came forth instantly. He didnt have to wait. Instead, results came forth as words were declared. In the glory realm, there is no waiting because waiting is a process in time, of which we have dominion over time; we operate outside the time dimension because we were given birth to in the eternal realm which falls outside our time dimension. The reason why some believers experience delays in their finances and manifestation of Miracle money is because of the absence of glory. The less you are filled with the glory, the longer it takes for you to cause Miracle money to manifest in the natural realm.

Because we have dominion over time, in the glory realm, you can declare Miracle money and use your royal prerogative to stipulate the time frame when it must manifest, where it should appear and in what amounts it should manifest. When the Bible attests that *you shall declare a thing and it shall be established for you*, it doesn't talk about flippantly declaring empty words in any direction but it talks about declaring things while in the glory realm or in an atmosphere of glory. That's when things happen. That is why those who function in higher realms of glory don't wait for things to happen, instead, they make things happen. This is because in the glory realm, it is possible for you to be instantaneously elevated to the reality of *overnight success*, whereby prayers are being answered even before you start praying. Let's look closely at how Ezekiel functioned on the prophetic glory:

> *So, I prophesied as I was commanded and as I prophesied, there was a noise, and suddenly a rattling and the bones came together bone to bone* (Ezekiel 37:7)

The instant Ezekiel prophesied, the noise began and the miracle started the moment the prophecy commenced. This is to tell you that prophecy does not just foretell; it creates that which is being said. It is the tool that brings it to pass. Confessing what you want God to do is different from declaring what He is saying right now while the glory is present. Both Elijah and Elisha walked and lived in the prophetic glory realm and when they spoke, it caused heaven and earth, kings and nations, to react and respond. They prophesied the opening of wombs, rain and drought, provisions, resurrections, and deaths, and the list goes on.

57. THE LAW OF DIVINE RESPONSE

Every created thing has sound waves and responds to sound waves spoken in the glory and Spirit of God

It is worth exploring the divine truth that when you speak words of faith directed by God in the glory realm, everything responds to your words. When you speak to Miracle money and command it to appear, it hears you and respond swiftly according to your word. The principle is that every created thing has sound waves and responds to sound waves spoken with the glory and Spirit of God. That is why Jesus spoke to a fig tree and commanded it to wither and it instantly responded because it was created with the capacity to hear and obey. Now, you understand why Jesus said we could speak to a mountain and it is possible for it to be removed (Mathew 17:20). The disciples also marvelled that *even the winds and the surging waters obey him*. The truth is that it's not only diseases that obeys and responds to our commands but the creation itself. Even Miracle money can be commanded to appear and swiftly come on feet in your direction and it will be established in the realm

Spiritual Laws & Principles of The Kingdom

of the spirit. Do you notice that God told Moses to speak to the rock so that it would produce water? This is the same principle of operating in the glory that we tap to when healing the sick. Because every body part and object of creation can hear and respond, when praying and commanding broken bones to reconnect, they can hear and respond just as all created things can. Likewise, Miracle money is manifested this way. This realisation opens a whole new world of authority over creation.

In the biblical account of creation, God spoke for the first time in recorded history in Genesis 1:3 saying, *"let there be light"* and instantly, there was light. Accordingly, everything was created with sound directing it to be a certain thing. This means that if you are in the glory of God, it is possible to redirect an object to be another created thing. If the original raw materials that created a certain object are present (Spirit), then sound can redirect the same created object into another form, especially if you are in the glory realm of God where the Spirit is hovering. The greater truth is that nothing created can be uncreated. According to the *law of thermodynamics*, things created only change form. For example, when you burn wood, it turns to ash but does not disappear completely. Although the ashes seem to dissolve, it is reduced to smaller molecules that still contain imbedded sound particles. This is to show you that one created object can turn into another created thing if directed by sound waves or commanded under the direction of the Holy Spirit.

How do you think Ezekiel was able to prophesy and speak to the bones such that they responded as a proof that they could hear and obey such that the sinews and flesh joined in and reformed? How could the flesh that was dissolved, rotten and now skeletons turn into an army? It's because nothing created is really gone even though it might have disappeared in the natural realm. It only changes form into smaller molecules and atoms we cannot see. It's just that it exists in another realm, in another form; hence, it can be brought back to its original form. Do you notice that Ezekiel even spoke to the dry bones' breath, which is the spirit such that it obeyed and returned? That is why when demonstrating Miracle money in the natural real, simply speak and command it to appear and it will be established. Imbued with this understanding, you realise that demonstrating Miracle money is certainly as easy as taking a walk through a park.

The greater truth is that creation responds to what human beings say or do. That's why the Bible says *the creation itself groans with birth pangs for the manifestation of the sons of God* (Romans 8:19, 22), meaning the earth is eagerly waiting for humanity to command it on what to do. Do you know that the Bible says money is crying out in the hands of those who use it for evil? As a believer, filled with the Spirit and inundated by the word of God, you have the authority over all creation and subjects in the natural realm, including Miracle money. In the same manner in which Jesus spoke to the billowing storms and boisterous winds of the sea, you can change weather patterns of geographical territories by speaking or commanding the winds, rain, sun (heat), and other physical phenomenon in the natural realm and they will obey you. By the same token, you can speak to financial storms to cease and command Miracle money to manifest in the natural realm and it will be done for you. For instance, when you wake up in the morning, you can command your morning and determine the exact financial conditions that you would want to see prevail in your life and neighbourhood and it shall be established.

To cement this divine truth with reference to further scriptural evidence, did you notice that the Bible says *the blood of Jesus speaks better things than that of Abel?* Do you notice in the context of the above scripture that the blood speaks? How possible is it that blood can speak? It's because it has sound waves and responds when commanded. In a similar vein, the Bible also mentions that *the blood of martyrs is crying out* (Genesis 4:10). We need to realise that all things have a voice and their sound can be carried over time to be experienced again. Are you not shocked that after more than 400 years, Elisha's bones still retained the anointing and the sound of God emanating from them such that a dead man who came into contact with Elisha's bones was raised back to life (2 Kings 13:21). This is to inspire you to get into the glory zone and speak Miracle money into visible manifestation and the creation will respond to your word.

58. THE LAW OF CONFESSION

The realm of glory is activated by spoken words.

It is a divine truth that Miracle money is a product of a spoken word. What you speak has such a tremendous effect on everything that you do. Speech is so powerful that it is recorded that everything was created by it. Speech was one of the first ingredients that created everything else you see and the invisible things you don't see. In the beginning the Creator spoke in Genesis 1: 3, saying *"let there be light"*, and light came forth instantaneously. The truth is that when you speak over the airwaves, you are invading and taking back the space of, *"the Prince of the power of the air"*, and displacing the enemy so that God can rule over the airwaves and bring His purposes to pass. From a scientific point of view, sound waves created by speech are so small that if you were to divide the smallest particles and atoms into some of the smallest forms inside them, at their core you would find vibration waves called *quarks*. From this scientific reality, comes a spiritual truth that sound waves are embedded in everything on earth, including rocks, food, trees and everything ever created. Therefore, these sounds waves can be altered and respond to other sound waves or speech. According to the studies conducted by a Japanese Researcher Masaru Emoto, water particles and other subatomic particles actually respond to sound and even speech or words spoken to them. If this is the case, then every created thing can hear in a sense and respond in some way, as they were first created with the same core ingredients – sound and light. This understanding can revolutionise your life, including the way you pray, minister and operate in the things of God.

In the light of the above, start to speak things you want to see manifested in your life. If you are going for a job interview, say that you are going to have favour with everyone you meet, and you will be successful. If you are sick, start telling your body that it is strong and healthy and that no sickness can survive in such a healthy state. Create your day each morning by speaking what you believe will be created that you will be successful in all that you do, that you are full of energy and this will cause things to shift from the invisible realm to the visible realm and will also take you from normal to supernatural. This is what we call *commanding your morning*. When you command your morning, you give your reality divine assignments and pull success from the spiritual realm into your day. On the basis of this principle, you can also speak to Miracle money and it will obey and appear wherever you want it to.

59. THE LAW OF DIVINE TRANSPORTATION

The glory travels through space and time.

The glory of God can be carried by invisible sound waves travelling through time and space. That is why it is possible for you to watch a miracle crusade on television that was filmed 3 months back and you receive Miracle money while watching it. It's because the glory has travelled through time and space to you. Even though you were not there when the actual crusade took place, whenever you watch it, the same glory is reactivated and you receive the same impartation of Miracle money as if you had been there 3 months ago. The glory of the meeting that took place at a particular time is frozen and reactivated the moment you watch it. So, the voice waves of the one speaking, the worship and the very atmosphere in that meeting can be contained in sound and light in the form of images and can be reactivated. That is why it is important to watch DVDs of anointed man of God because there is an impartation of Miracle money grace from these meetings frozen in time, waiting for you to receive it and release it by just pushing the play button of the DVD player.

This is the same principle by which the Bones of Elisha held a reservoir of glory and sound waves of power such that a man who was thrown into the same grave where Elisha had been buried more than four hundred years back was instantly resurrected (1 Kings 13:21). This is simply because the glory travels through space and time and in this case, it had travelled ahead more than four hundred into the future such that the same degree of resurrection glory which soaked into Elisha's body during his life time on earth was still present to raise the dead. As Elisha was now in a higher realm of glory in Heaven, his body was now the only point of contact to transmit the glory between Heaven and earth. This is what we call *Elisha glory,* when a torch of the last generation is passed to the next generation with even greater power. This is to tell you that the glory travels through time and space, which is why in in the glory realm, one can be divinely transported in the spirit dimension to other places just like the experience of Philip in Azotus. That is why multitudes of believers shall experience *divine transportation* in the spirit in the end times days.

60. THE LAW OF DOMINION OVER THE TIME FACTOR

The realm of glory falls outside the time dimension in the natural realm, hence functioning in that realm grants us dominion over time.

It is worth exploring the divine truth that as believers, we have authority over time, hence we can command Miracle money to manifest in the now or at whatever time we want it to appear and it will be established in the realm of the spirit. This is because time is not one of the characteristics of God. God is not defined by time because He lives, functions and operates in the eternal realm that is outside our time dimension. Time is not an absolute because it only exists when its parameters are defined by absolutes. God set the earth in time while man was created from the eternal realm. Although man lives on earth, he doesn't operate according to earthly time because he was created in the eternal realm which falls outside the scope or domain of time. Man was never designed to function according to earthly time. It was only after the fall that the clock started ticking. Heaven is governed by the glory which is the realm of eternity where there is no time. Therefore, when we are caught up into the glory, we experience *"timelessness"*. The eternity realm is the womb from which time came. In other words, eternity existed before time. Time is the offspring of the eternal design. Time was created or set in creation after eternity on the fourth day. God set the sun to rule by day and the moon to rule by night, thereby establishing time and season. That is why we have dominion over time because we were created first in the eternal realm which is outside the time dimension of the earth.

With this understanding therefore, when operating in the realm of glory, the key is to learn the art of how to speak from the eternal realm into the realm of time. In the gory realm, time does not exist as we consider it on earth. The only thing that can break the cycle of time is faith. Faith is a higher law than time. It is the ascent out of time into the eternal realm. For a man who knows his rights as a citizen of Heaven, time is made to serve him. Man was not designed to serve time. Time is a part of matter, not a matter of time. Faith is God's matter - the substance or material which represents elements which are made by God to serve an eternal purpose. Time was designed and created specifically for this earth. It doesn't exist outside this planet. The reality is that when people loose track of time and step into the eternal, the eternal becomes real and the supernatural becomes your normal. In this Kairos moment, God is bridging you from time into the eternal realm whereby it is naturally supernatural to perform miracles. That's when you will realise that the eternal is more real than time. The truth is that miracles are in a higher realm, without the influence of time, while our circumstances are the product of time with a beginning and an end.

61. THE LAW OF DIVINE SPEED AND ACCELERATION

The realm of glory is a realm of divine speed and acceleration.

Apostle Frequency Revelator

It is worth exploring the divine truth that speed and acceleration are key processes involved in the manifestation of Miracle money in the natural realm because God's work needs to be accomplished with a sense of urgency in this season. As the Body of Christ, we are about to enter a new season in Church history, a phase that goes beyond the initial Pentecostal experience. When this glory invasion is fully realised, it will usher in a supernatural acceleration of the things of God. To substantiate this truth with reference to a quintessential example, Elijah prayed and saw the first sign as small as a man's hand and the Bible says when he saw it, he gird his loins and outran King Ahab's horse which was probably the fastest and best fed horse in the country. But how possible is it that a man can outrun a horse while he is on foot? Running is a prophetic sign, symbolic of divine speed and acceleration in the realm of the spirit. That was a *dramatic prophetic gesture*. It was a prophetic action of faith, symbolic of how we should move in the spirit dimension to overtake things in the natural realm. While he was seen sprinting in the natural realm, in the spirit realm, that was actually an action of faith. When you read this portion of scripture with the eyes if flesh, you will see Elijah running in the natural realm but if you read with the eye of the spirit, you will see him flying in the spirit. This is a dimension in the spirit called *Holy Ghost transportation*. Elijah was catapulted into a higher realm of glory and divinely transported through the tidal waves of the spirit to Jezreel. Prophetically speaking, as God has already unveiled the first sign of the *glory cloud* heralding a new outpouring of glory in the realm of the spirit, now is the time to run in the dimension of the spirit. As Elijah did, pick up your loins and run so as not to miss the next move of God. Don't just casually walk towards it, but run so you don't miss it. This is the season of the *overtaking anointing*. It's time that you run ahead of everything which represents Ahab's horse in your life.

Did you know that when you are operating in the glory realm, which is outside our time dimension you can actually overtake time in the natural realm. You have two options when operating in the glory realm; it's either you stop the time until you have completed certain divine tasks as exemplified by Joshua or you can simply overtake it. When we stop the cloak, we step backwards in time but when we overtake it, we step forward. That is why the Bible concurs that in this *Kairos* moment, we have unequivocally stepped into Amos 9:13— a critical moment in which *the ploughman is overtaking the reaper and the treader of grapes him that sows a seed*. While the *Reaper* is harvesting as fast as he can, on his heels comes the *Ploughman,* who is already preparing another harvest in the soil that the reaper has just harvested. This infers that in this final chapter of human history, all of eternity is pouring into the present, causing us to accelerate forward. In other words, we have entered *the rush hour* of God, a critical moment in God's calendar in which things are moving so fast in the realm of the spirit as we are adjourning quickly towards the second coming of the Lord, Jesus Christ. The truth is that the glory is an accelerator; hence what would normally take years happens in a moment in the gory realm. Those who don't understand the operation of the glory realm are forced to wait for the date the doctor has set for them to receive their healing. This is an error because the glory realm is a realm of speed and acceleration where there is neither procrastination, postponement nor delays. If the doctor has told you to wait for six months, just defy the law of time and activate the higher law of faith; reach into the future and take your healing right now!

62. THE LAW OF DIVINE REVELATION

The realm of glory is a realm of revelation.

It is worth exploring the divine truth that Miracle money is a product of revelation, which is given birth to in the deeper territories of the glory realm. The glory realm itself is also a realm of revelation. It is a realm whereby everything is known. It is beyond the realm of gifts, faith and the anointing. Figuratively speaking, common sense is to the natural man what revelation is to the man in the Glory of God. Revelation comes before manifestation and without revelation there is no acceleration of the manifestation. By the same token, without revelation, Miracle money cannot be demonstrated in the natural realm. Hypothetically speaking, you cannot get fire from water; it takes fire to set a fire in the same way it takes a certain amount of rain to cause a flood. By the same token, without a constant flow of revelation, manifestation will not tarry. *The glory realm is a realm of Revelation.* That is why there is such a thing as *the revelation glory*. This involves allowing God to speak to our spirit when we are basking in the atmosphere of His glory. It incorporates seeing things materialise before they happen and witnessing things happening while they are being spoken. In the spirit realm, unless something is revealed, it remains a mystery. The Bible concurs with the divine truth that *it is the glory of God to conceal a thing but the honour of kings to search out a matter* (Proverbs 25:2). It is important to unveil the divine truth that Miracle money is manifested through *revelation*. Unless and if you have a personal revelation of what miracle money is, where it comes from, how it operates and manifest, it might not be possible for you to manifests it. I'm not talking about saying what a pastor has said or trying to do what you have seen men of God doing but I'm talking about receiving your own revelation from God concerning Miracle money. The reason why certain miracles do not happen is because people do not have a personal revelation of how to operate or flow in them. This is why God is looking for a distinct calibre of believers whom He shall breed His presence, to ignite the passion for progressive revelation in this end times.

The greater truth is that what is revelatory to the Heavens is prophetic to the earth. The distinguishing characteristic feature of the glory realm is that things in the Heavens are not learned but they are just known or revealed. It is not possible to study and learn the revelatory realm. It must be revealed and this explains why Paul wrote three quarters of the New Testament when in actual fact he never went to a Bible school. It is possible to learn the operation of the prophetic realm, but not the revelatory realm. There is a world of difference between the *revelatory* and the *prophetic experience*. They are governed by different rules, as the one originates from the throne of Glory, and the other originates from this fallen atmosphere. The truth is that Heaven operates in present tense, while the earth has different time zones or tenses. Here, we have the past, present and future perfect tense. If anything comes to the earth from the Heavens, it has to fit into one of these three tenses in order to remain in the earth and manifest in these three dimensional realms. It has come into the earth, leave the realm of eternity from whence it came and penetrate the realm of time. For this to happen, it must be framed, or claimed by the words of our mouth. Then it remains in our time zone, and will manifest to us in the natural realm. In view of the above, it is therefore scripturally evident that revelation is such an indispensable necessity to unlocking the supernatural doors to abundance. Without revelation, Miracle money remains a mystery and God's people remain trapped in a morass of debilitating poverty.

63. THE LAW OF **DIVINE ORCHESTRATION**

The glory realm is the birthplace for all creation; everything was created from the realm of glory.

It is a divine truth that Miracle money is a product of God's glory as it originates in the glory realm. Before the beginning began, God existed. He always was eternal. Before the beginning, there was nowhere for Him to come from. This is why He had to create "*the beginning*". While the majority of believers seem to subscribe to this divine truth, some folks erroneously believe that God created the earth out of nothing and that everything came out of the blue, out of the invisible matter. No! That is not the correct picture because everything He created was already in Him. So, when He spoke, and said *let there be light,* light proceeded from within the depths of His being into manifestation in the natural realm. That is why with an indwelling presence of the Holy Spirit, everything you will ever need in life is in you. Therefore, we follow the same pattern which God used to speak things from within our being into existence. Isn't it amazing that God created all things out of himself? As He called, *light be,* light came forth from the depth of His being into existence. When God said, *Let there be light,* what came forth was the voice of the almighty penetrating the vastness of His perception in the eternal realm as He spoke into existence that which He had already created within His being. The very essence of His thought life was thrust into existence, and seen when He spoke. Thoughts became words, words became objective reality. All He had to do was to call out of Himself those things which were a part of His glory and they responded. The sound of His voice preceded the visible manifestation of each creative work. In this final chapter of human history, the lion of the tribe of Judah is therefore roaring again, unleashing the sound of heaven on earth through the end time generation. It could therefore be deduced that everything that you will ever need in this life, be it miracles, finances, healings, prosperity, is available in the glory realm. Therefore, tap into the atmosphere of glory to speak anything that you want to see happen in this world and it shall be established for you.

In view of the above, it is worth exploring the divine truth that the Glory realm is the realm of our birth; it's where we were born into the glory. That's were our true identity and origin is. We were created in the realm of glory. We are from there. Our origin is in the glory, in the Heavenly realm. By the same token, Miracle money also originates from the same realm. Heaven is the only place in eternity that is named, and yet, Heaven is created. Heaven is the Capital of the Eternal Realm that is why it is a city. To elucidate more on this divine truth, the Bible speaks of *three* Heavens. The *first Heaven* is the atmosphere around the earth. The *second Heaven* is the atmosphere where Lucifer and his fallen angels were assigned to exist, between the third Heaven and the earth. The *third Heaven* is where we find God's throne room. This is where the Glory of God dwells. This is where we originated. This atmosphere is where we long to be, because it is where we came from. Therefore, when we get hungry for the presence of God, we are actually homesick for the atmosphere He created us in.

Apostle Frequency Revelator

Have you ever asked God to take you back in time through the spirit dimension to an epic era before conception when you were a created spirit before His throne? Only in that realm would you fully comprehend that you were created in the *Throne Room* of Heaven. The reality is that when we are born again, God places His glory in our spirit so that we receive the divine "*breath of life*" and His spiritual DNA. God's DNA contains His glory as His son Jesus. Before being born again, we had Adam's sinful DNA, but now we have God's sanctified DNA hence, we can always carry the glory of God wherever we go. However, the greatest challenge facing us as believers is that we are more comfortable talking about the anointing, instead of manifesting the glory, which is denotes our birth place in the spirit realm. We have already been in this realm before. We were created there. Now, we must learn how to access it once again, and re-enter its atmosphere. That is why Paul uses the phrase "*Whom He foreknew*" to show that we have known this glory realm before. We have functioned and operated in it before the foundations of the earth. Now, we are just replaying the tap in which we have featured as actors before and acting like a man trampling on his own footsteps where he had walked before.

CHAPTER SIX

THE HIGHER LAWS OF FINANCIAL PROSPERITY

What Divine Principles Can We Take Advantage of In Order To Rain Down Miracle Money from Heaven?

In order to have an in-depth understanding of the dynamics of Miracle money, it is imperative that you secure a revelation of the higher laws of finance because Miracle money is accessed not based on what you have done but on the grace of God. In our endeavour to pursue the end time financial prosperity agenda and amass humungous financial wealth from Heaven, it is vital that we introspect ourselves and relook into our theology to see from a different light if there is something relating to ministry that we cannot see clearly. Amongst these things which should be re-looked into is what I call *higher laws of finance*. Apparently, preachers and ministers of the gospel have always customarily over emphasized the *law of sowing and reaping* above all other laws as a prime law by which God prospers His people. In some cases the survival of pastors depends on the message they preach, hence there is a tendency to over emphasise certain portions of scripture especially where money is concerned. It is a typical scenario in some charismatic cycles to find Christians who sow and then claim a hundred fold increase in return to what they would have sown in hope that whatever they sow would bring forth a bumper harvest, yet there are other *higher laws of finance* which believers could apply in order to reap the same bumper harvest quickly and bountifully. It is worth exploring the divine truth that Miracle money is not a product of sowing and reaping. In other words, you don't have to sow in order to reap Miracle money. Instead, it is based on higher laws of finance which places a recipient in a position of favour, to receive from God even without doing anything to reciprocate His gesture of love. Millions of believers in the Body of Christ are rigorously engaged in sowing and reaping in the hope of becoming millionaires but the sober truth is: How many of them are Millionaires? Very few! Why? Because there is more to the realm of God's prosperity than sowing and reaping which is a basic, entry level law in the realm of prosperity. Three higher laws of finance seem to surface with regard to the practical demonstration of Miracle money in this last season shortly before the Master comes back for the Grand Finale of the earth. And these are, *the law of reaping where you did not sow, the law of buying without money and the law of binding and loosing money.*

THE LAW OF REAPING WHERE YOU DID NOT SOW

One striking reality is that as I assiduously examined the scriptures and analytically looked at all the laws of finance which have been brought forth and overemphasized by modern day preachers, God began to show me something from a different light. There is a higher law of finance than what preachers have over emphasized and this is *the law of reaping where you did not sow*. Notable is the realisation that in the realm of God, there are *greater truths* and *lesser truths*. By the same token, there are *higher laws* and *lesser laws* of finance. The law of sowing and reaping is a lesser law while the notion of *reaping where you did not sow* is a higher law. Prophetically speaking, taking into account the nature of the end time season in which we have been ushered as per God's calendar, we no longer just rely only on the law of sowing and reaping as a key determinant for our financial prosperity. If God were to wait for the church to reap what we sow, it would take a considerable length of time for the church to reap everything He wants us to reap before the Lord

Spiritual Laws & Principles of The Kingdom

Jesus Christ comes back. Even if it's a hundred fold harvest, the church will not be able to reap all that which Jesus wants us to experience or be blessed with before His second coming. If God were to rely just on what we sow, the church of Jesus Christ may never reach the fullness of what God wants us to receive. Notable is the fact that if we only reap what we sow, there is a sense in which it is limited to our own works. Therefore, there has to be a higher law of finance that comes forth like a booster, which God has provided to expedite His divine plans and purpose in this end time season which marks the conclusion of His eternal plan on earth.

It is for this reason that in this end time season, God is propagating the grace for Miracle Money so as to speed up His divine plans and purpose concerning financial prosperity and provision. The release of Miracle Money is therefore what I call *a practical demonstration of signs and wonders in the arena of our finances*. It is unequivocally evident that God uses Miracle money for His children to catch up where they have lacked behind financially. So, Miracle money is a catalyst that speed up the rate at which finances are supernaturally dispatched in the natural realm to expedite God's purpose. Prophetically speaking, in this season of Miracle money, the Lord shall accelerate you to your divine destiny, the gravity of faith shall propel you into the future and the power of the Spirit shall catapult you to highest realms of Glory whereby you shall amass humongous financial wealth from Heaven like a farmer sent out to the field for a bumper harvest. What could have taken you months of sowing and reaping will be manifested in a flip of a moment; what could have taken you years of toiling and labouring to accomplish; you will achieve it in few minutes; and what could have taken you years of studying and researching to figure out; will be revealed in a twinkling of an eye. This is to tell you that speed and acceleration are twin processes behind the manifestation of our financial breakthrough in this critical season. It should come to no surprise that your life is programmed to move progressively in one direction, upward and forward only. There is no reverse gear to your walk of faith with God. There is neither a bus stop, parking lot nor road block in your journey into the spirit dimension. Pertaining to the pursuit of His end time financial prosperity agenda, the Lord once said that,

> *"I desire to do signs and wonders in the finances of every one of My children, because they've been so far behind. The only way I can really bring them up in their finances before Jesus comes is to do miracles, signs and wonders in their finances."* God said, *"I'm going to do a quick work in order to get the money back into the hands of My children. I'm going to show signs and wonders in the arena of finances,*

Apostle Frequency Revelator

because My people have been lagging behind for too long. Those who will take Me at My Word, I'm going to do a quick work in their finances."

This is to tell you how expedient it is to be catapulted into the realm of Kingdom millionaires to fulfil God's plan in this end time season. As far as God is concerned, miracles, signs, and wonders are the only means for believers to catch up to where He has always wanted them to be in terms of their financial prosperity. Therefore, He will do whatever it takes to ensure that they are brought to that realm of plenty. In other words, in the same way God took Paul and Silas out of prison with speed and haste (Acts 16:16-40), He is going to do some things *"immediately"* and *"suddenly"* in people's lives to provide a supernatural escape from poverty and lack into a realm of super abundance. Owing to lack of revelation, many people have always thought that signs and wonders are only about lame people walking again, the blind receiving their sight, deaf ears being opened and the dead being raised but God wants to perform signs and wonders in people's *finances* too. In other words, in this season, we don't have enough time left for us to go the old confession route. Certainly, we have to maintain our faith and our confession but in this end time season, God is going to add a *booster* to our confession so that we can experience a torrent of miracles, signs, and wonders in our finances. God said, "I will do a *quick* work with their money so that they will know that it is of Me. Philosophically speaking, if you could think of the speed of a jet plane flying overhead, that is how fast things are going to happen in many people's finances. And if you could think of the number of stars in the sky on a clear night, that is how much money He's going to pour on the members of the Body of Christ who steadfastly hold on to this divine revelation. However, the power to create miracles, signs and wonders in your finances will not be activated until you learn to depend totally on God's Word. More so, your faith has to be unhindered by religious beliefs and misconstrued traditions of the past that you have perhaps been holding on to.

It is imperative that in order to receive a humongous financial breakthrough and millions of wealth in our lives, we need to practically demonstrate signs and wonders in our finances. This is in view of the fact that as much as money is natural, on the other side of the coin, it is also spiritual. The Bible concurs with this revelation as it asserts that the *things which are seen are made out of the things which are not seen* (Hebrews 11:3). That means there is an original blue print of money in all currencies of this world in the realm of the spirit. Therefore, in order to release money which is a spiritual subject, we need to practically demonstrate signs and wonders in our finances so that money can come swiftly and speedily from the realm of the spirit into the realm of the natural. However, it is disheartening to note that while multitudes of Christians have tapped into the realm of demonstrating the power of God in healings, miracles and deliverance, very few hardly get to think about demonstrating signs and wonders in their finances yet this is critical in the release of our millions of wealth in this present time. It is for this reason that as part of the last wave of prosperity in this end time season, God uses Miracle money to bless His children so that it can be ingrained in their thinking that money is spiritual. Hence, in order to cause its abundant and humongous manifestation in the natural realm, signs and wonders must be demonstrated in our finances.

It is worth exploring the divine truth that speed and acceleration are crucial ingredients which characterises the move of the Spirit in this end time season. In other words, there is a heightened degree of acceleration in the realm of God's financial prosperity. The Lord showed me recently in an encounter how time is running out and eternity is rushing in. In this experience, I began to understand how in the Book of Amos, the ploughman could overtake the reaper—the eternal realm was literally overtaking time in the natural. As the Body of Christ, we are standing at the threshold of a new era—the brink of a new age. The power for acceleration is in the timeless realm of God's Glory. When the realm of the Glory of God moves into the realm of the natural, there comes a great acceleration for financial prosperity and the release of creative power to create wealth. It is vital to step into maturity—as you encounter new realms of God's supernatural financial provision. Therefore, in this end time season, seeds of destiny are ready for reaping. The Lord has shown me that we are in this time of acceleration; we have stepped into Amos 9:13—*"the ploughman will overtake the reaper."* All of eternity is pouring into the present causing us to accelerate forward. Seeds that have been sown in the past, seeds of destiny, are full-grown and ready for reaping. As the realm of eternity is meshed with the present, we are witnessing a culmination of events—loose ends are being tied up before the return of Christ. Things that would normally take ten years to happen will only take ten months—even ten weeks. There is a rapid maturity taking place in the Body of Christ as the cloud of His presence descends and blankets us corporately. This season is not simply coming—it is here!

Therefore, in this critical season, God has reserved this truth and understanding that it is not by works but by grace of God that we will be able to enter into the realm of supernatural financial prosperity that God wants us to step into. In this season, you don't just reap what you sow but you reap what Jesus sowed. It is on the basis of this revelation that many believers shall reap humungous wealth from Heaven and be elevated into the realm of Kingdom millionaires even without sowing anything. Therefore, in this season, God is saying to us,

> *"Come up higher in your finances there is a higher law of finance which you can tap into.*

Contrary to how dozens of preachers have stigmatised it, sowing and reaping is an entry level, training phase or elementary truth in the realm of God's financial prosperity and abundance. The greater truth is that all those things which we have learnt in sowing and reaping are just an epitome of God' training ground for us so that upon maturity, we can progress or migrate to God's higher laws of financial prosperity. God wants to elevate and awaken us to a higher law, which is learning to reap not what we sow but what Jesus sowed. This is such a powerful revelation which if understood across the Body of Christ, shall unreservedly release the superabundance that God has determined for you in this end time season. The question you are probably asking yourself is: *But what did Jesus sow?* He sowed His entire being and whole life -- everything that He had, everything that He represented when He came here to earth, He laid it at the cross as a seed and sowed for us. Therefore, one of the notable blessings of the finished works of Christ is that it has now ushered us into a realm of superabundance and thus, put a definite halt to a life of untold hardship, fruitless toils and bitter experiences. And if every believer could get this spiritual reality engrained in their thinking that Jesus freely sowed for us to reap bountifully, then practically demonstrating millions in Miracle money will be a walk through a park.

To cement this revelation with reference to scriptural evidence, in Deuteronomy 6:10, it is strikingly interesting to note what God said to the children of Israel just before they went into the land of Canaan.

> *God promised to give them cities which they did not built, wells which they did not dig, and vine yards which they did not plant.*

It is evident on the basis of the above mentioned scriptural evidence that obviously the promise of the land of Canaan was not reaped because of what they sow. Instead, it was reaping a promise and blessing which God had given to Abraham. If they had to reap what they sow for Israelites to enter into the land of Canaan, it would have been very meagre because most of the time they were complaining and grumbling against God. They did not know how to sow yet they were reaping and they didn't even reap what they deserved. Instead, they got everything that they obtained by the grace of God. No way could they have reaped what they sowed in such a huge expanse of Canaan. So, they reaped what Abraham sowed as they looked forward in time to the coming of the Lord Jesus Christ to earth. This divine truth is corroborated by the Apostle John's remark that *I sent you to reap that which you have not laboured: others have laboured, and you have entered into their labour* (John 4:38 (ASV). It is interesting to note that the act of reaping here is tied to Abraham, Isaac and Jacob, in what we call the *Abrahamic covenant*. When God spoke to Abraham that was way back in Genesis 12, where He said *in you shall all the families of the earth be blessed* (Genesis 22:18), it was this blessing given to Abraham which the Children of Israel later reaped without doing anything or working for it. When God said to Abraham all the families of the earth shall be blessed through you, He meant that Abraham was now being bequeathed the inheritance of the entire world which Adam lost to the devil in the playground of the Garden of Eden. In Galatians 3:13-14, Paul tells us that Jesus was hung on the cross so that all the blessings of Abraham might gravitate upon us through the Holy Spirit. Imbued with this understanding, you suddenly realise that as a seed of Abraham, the whole world is yours and that all the silver and gold, measured by the best currencies of the world, are yours to unreservedly indulge.

It is unequivocally evident that everything which Jesus sowed for us have to be reaped by the church before it is taken out by the rapture. Therefore, let's move into the *higher laws of finance* and not just depend on what we sow. However, I'm not ruling out the idea that people should give but I'm awakening believers to the divine consciousness that they are levels in which divine truths are ranked in the spirit as there are greater truths and lesser truths. I believe a hundred fold is a fantastic law but God wants to accelerate the manifestation of His blessings as we step into the higher realm of believing what Jesus has sown. Thank God for the entry level principle of sowing and reaping but due to the urgency and perspicacity with which divine tasks have to be executed in this season, you need to go further than the basics of the law of sowing and reaping and begin to declare that *I'm going to reap what Jesus sowed*. By so doing, you will be thrilled at how you shall trigger a heavy torrential downpour of God's financial rain in your life. In Galatians 3, Paul expounds on the prophecy that *Abraham will be the heir to the world* when he says *to the Seed he will give* and the word "*Seed*" has a capital letter "*S*" which denotes the person of Jesus. Subsequently, Jesus came to the world, died on the cross and fulfilled the promise such that the whole world through the precious blood of Jesus Christ now by legal spiritual transaction belong to Jesus and Satan and his cohorts have been reduced to zero and legally they have no more rights to this earth. This debunks the wayward mentality of the devil's crowd that he can give Miracle money. How can the devil give something that he doesn't even have? In Galatians 3: 8, Paul unveils the fact that *those who are of faith are blessed through their divine connection to Abraham.* The truth is that as a born again believer, you are called and separated unto the blessing of God. Therefore, you don't have to do anything to be blessed; just because you are in Christ, you are in Abraham and you are already blessed. Through the revelation that Jesus has sown for us and has paid the price for the entire world, we now reap or partake of all the blessings which Christ has brought through His precious blood, hence there is not even one single thing we need to do to reciprocate the blessing. In a sense, you don't have to sow in order to receive because Jesus has already sown for us. All other spiritual exercises such as prayer and fasting, we do them not because we want to reap what we have sown but we want to align our spirits so that we can move swiftly in the spirit dimension to get hold of what is already ours. As far as God is concerned, spiritual exercises such as fasting, prayer, giving are elementary truths or teachings of the gospel. The law of sowing and reaping was originally designed to teach us this principle. It is an elementary teaching. It works just like how we teach a child. In order to train a child, you start with the fundamentals or basics and once the child has learnt and grasped these, only then would you move to solid staff. In the same way, sowing and reaping as a spiritual law was originally designed to teach us what Jesus has done. All these laws are essential as they tell us in a little picture what God has done in a big picture but the sad thing is that many believers get stuck in the lesser and lower laws such that they don't realise that there is a higher law up there that is already been fulfilled for us. The law of sowing and reaping was a small picture of the biggest seed of what God has done. God has sown Jesus for us for He died so that we might receive all the fullness of His blessings and that is *the higher law of finance.* And when we understand that, the next question would be: *How do we tap into this higher law?*

In a practical sense, you must not just believe God based on what you are, what you have or what you can do because there is a sense in which that is tied to your own works. Instead, believe God based on what Jesus had done. Jesus has sown in an unlimited measure, hence we just to have faith to rise and take what Jesus has freely done for us. God can move us into a higher realm to receive by His grace what we cannot receive by our works. The minute we believe that we are entitled to receive from God based on what we have done, we shut ourselves against the covenant of grace. One other striking reality is that the law of sowing and reaping operates for all human beings whether they know God or not. It is as workable as the law of gravity, it affects both Christians and non–Christians. That means non-Christians who actually sow, do reap too and that explains why some of them are wealthy even if they do not know God. It is therefore not good enough for Christians to solitarily rely on a law that works for everybody because I believe that there should be a demarcation line that clearly distinguish between Christians and non-Christians. Partaking in the portion of unbelievers through sharing the same level of grace is not good enough. However, for those who have a blood covenant, there is a higher law of reaping what Jesus sowed and this is a higher law which Jesus wants to bring us into in this season that will clearly distinguish between believers from unbelievers. That is why God is populating this world with Miracle money as a mark of distinction engraved upon His chosen ones.

Now, the question is: *How does this higher law operate*? The answer is simple! By accepting and embracing everything Jesus has done for you on the cross and freely positioning yourself to receive and partake of the blessings which are legally and rightfully yours. This is done through the dynamic working of the Spirit, intimacy with God through spiritual encounters, the degree of manifestation of God's presence and deep expressions of faith. Therefore, if you want to function in the arena of God's unlimited financial prosperity, just plunge yourself into the greater depths of God's presence to access the unlimited financial blessings and you will be instantly catapulted into the realm of millionaires. According to Galatians 3:14, when you exercise faith in God, you receive it through the Spirit. Your spiritual capacity to receive or the extent to which your spirit man is developed is what determines how much of God's financial provision you can receive and not how much you have sown. It is through the Spirit of God which illuminates a revelation in your spirit and drops a spiritual substance that you are able to produce the wealth according to the grace God has for your life. Therefore, let's migrate to higher laws of finance which Paul describes as weightier matters of the Kingdom. When the whole Body of Christ catches this revelation, we will be able to believe God not just based on what we have or what we are able to sow. This is what will provoke an avalanche of the river of Miracle money, streaming copiously from the Throne Room of Heaven, to precipitate upon the masses who are connected to God's grace in the natural realm. Therefore all the **SEVEN** dimensions of supernatural financial prosperity such as *Miracle money, Wealth transfer, Supernatural Debt cancellation, Supernatural multiplication* *of wealth, the golden rain, Supernatural Recreation of substances and Reclamation of lost property* are not based on the law of sowing and reaping but on the higher laws of financial prosperity because you have full access to partake of their portion even without sowing anything. They are accessed based on the availability of God's grace, glory and degree of manifestation of His presence and not how much you have sown.

THE LAW OF BUYING WITHOUT MONEY

Have you ever walked into a shop and bought things without paying for them, or you were at the airport and while waiting in the queue to pay for the ticket, somebody else pays for you or you were in a restaurant and while waiting to pay the bill, somebody else settles it on your behalf or you were at a fuel station and while you wait to pay for your full tank, somebody interrupts you and pay the cost? If yes, then you will easily understand this divine principle of buying without money. By buying without money, I don't mean walking into a supermarket and using your faith to pay for your groceries. No! I mean being in a situation when you are expected to pay for a service rendered or a product bought, then all of a sudden, someone appears from nowhere and pays for you. This is highly attributable to the work of angels in the invisible realm in which a supernatural influence is released in the realm of the spirit that compels forces of divinity to work on your behalf. This is a higher law of finance because through it is the grace of God exhibited to its highest degree, without any reservations. There are divine arrangement of circumstances in the realm of the spirit that causes Heaven's attention to be directed towards you such that you just find yourself in a situation in which people are paying things for you, without necessarily having to ask them to. This is still Miracle money but manifesting in another form. Its Miracle money in the sense that there is a monetary value attached to what you could have paid but then by God's grace, somebody else is paying for you.

This is what Jesus described in prophetic language as *"Buying without Money"*. Jesus made a public declaration saying *"Hey there! All who are thirsty, come to the water! Are you penniless? Come anyway—buy and eat! Come, buy your drinks, buy wine and milk. Buy without money—everything's free! Why do you spend your money on junk food, your hard-earned cash on cotton candy? Listen to me, listen well: Eat only the best, fill yourself with only the finest. Pay attention, come close now, listen carefully to my life-giving, life-nourishing words* (Isaiah 55:1). Although this revelation was spoken in the context of salvation, there is a sense in which it relates to

Spiritual Laws & Principles of The Kingdom

God's supernatural financial provision. It is irrefutably evident in this season of Miracle money that Jesus is re-echoing the same words which He uttered thousands of years back and He is calling men and woman to step out of the level of impossibility thinking to a realm of superabundance in which they unreservedly partake of His grace without paying anything. Do you notice the language of money which Jesus uses in the above-mentioned portion of scripture? He says, *Buy without money—everything's free!* Clearly, He is not talking about buying the anointing, power or healing here because these ones cannot be commoditized as they are rendered free of charge. Instead, He is talking about Miracle money which He is freely pouring out upon the masses who accept and embrace His saving grace in the light of His creation. Consider the rhetoric question which Jesus is asking you in this season: *Why do you spend your hard-earned cash on cotton candy?* Isn't it interesting to note that Jesus is against the idea of you spending your hard-earned money on things which you could easily obtain using Miracle money? This is to tell you how eager Jesus is to ease your burden so that you don't labor and toil from dusk till dawn for the substance of money when you can receive it supernaturally. In the realm of the spirit, a door has been wide opened and Jesus is saying, *"Come, you who do not have money, come eat and drink"*. Do you notice that in the context of this scripture, what Jesus is saying here is that He wants to give you money so that you can pay all your bills? Depending on the amount received, some recipients of Miracle Money will use it to for Kingdom expansion purposes such as building churches, conference centres, sponsoring Kingdom projects, taking care of the needy and orphans while others will use it to simply pay their bills and cover their debts. [1]This is the extent to which Miracle money shall be widely manifested in this season. In view of the above scripture, people tend to ask a question, *"Can God give anybody money without working for it?"* Emphatically, Yes! He can because He is revealing to us His integral role as the father who cares for His children. Miracle money is given by God free of charge, even without working for it or paying for it or doing anything but it's a manifestation of God's grace as a way of showing deep love and care to His people. In this regard, an open invitation is still being made by God through the angels, calling men and women to step up in faith to freely access the grace which He has reserved for His children. Miracle money is one of those free gifts which God wants His children to partake of in these end times.

THE LAW OF BINDING AND LOOSING MONEY

It must be understood that Money is not just a theoretical concept but a practical phenomenon. In your quest to becoming Kingdom Millionaires and Billionaires, you must make a practical demonstration by commanding money into existence. It is disheartening to note that multitudes of believers continues to enjoy the limited outer court of God's blessings and while some might have received *some* return on their giving and experienced *some* financial blessings, the truth is that we haven't gotten our money loosed yet as we ought. Did you know that the precipitation of Miracle money in the natural realm is a product of the binding and loosing processes that takes place in the realm of the spirit? The greater truth is that binding and loosing is a higher law of finance which works like a double-edged-sword that dismantles the walls of lack, insufficiency and poverty while at the same time releasing abundance into our lives. It is worth exploring the divine truth that during Miracle money demonstrations, we must loose Miracle money in the same manner in which we loose our healing. It is of paramount significance to highlight as an introductory perspective to this revelation the fact that many of the scriptures which multitudes of Christians rely on for the exercise of their healing can actually be used to loose money.

To cement this revelation with reference to scriptural evidence, Jesus declared in Mathew 18:18, that, *"Verily I say unto you, whatsoever you shall bind on earth shall be bound in Heaven, and whatsoever you shall loose on earth shall be loosed in Heaven"*. Unknown to many folks, this is a higher law of finance in the sense that it authorises the instantaneous release of our finances whenever it is demonstrated in the natural realm. In the context of the above-mentioned scripture, the word "loose" means *to let go, untie, release* and *set free*. This means that through the knowledge of God's Word and His will concerning your prosperity, you can *bind* poverty and lack in your life and *loose* or *release* divine prosperity and abundance. Moreover, the word *"whatsoever"* means anything. Well, does *"anything"* include money? Certainly, it does! It doesn't make any difference what it is, whether it is healing or money or deliverance —if you loose it, Jesus said, *"I'll* loose it." Do you realize what Jesus is saying? First, He is saying, in effect, "Whatever is loosed in your life is going to be loosed because *you're* doing the loosing, not Me. It's not up to Me to loose it first. *You* are to 'call the shots.' But when you loose something according to My Word, no one can stop it from being loosed"! Therefore, whether you loose hundreds, thousands, millions or billions in Miracle money into your account, the

Spiritual Laws & Principles of The Kingdom

bottom line is that they shall be loosed regardless of quantity.

The other reason why this is a higher law of finance is because it enables us to operate from a higher Heavenly realm in which we are able to bind any demonic principalities responsible for the interception of our finances from the spirit realm into the natural realm. Colloquially speaking, in the spirit realm, when you say" *I bind you devourer of my finances,*" you can literally see a string coming and tying down those devils. In a similar vein, if you say to money, *"Money cometh into my bank account now,"* because you are releasing it, you can literally see piles of paper money in all the currencies of the world raining down upon you. Moreover, in the context of our opening scripture above, Jesus said, *"I'll loose it in Heaven,"* Note that He is not talking about loosing something in Heaven. Yes, Jesus is in Heaven, but He is "loosing" *from* Heaven, not *in* Heaven. He is speaking of releasing your blessing from a Heavenly realm where you are seated with Him at the right hand of God. As aforementioned, in Heaven, your blessings won't need to be loosed, because they are not bound up! No, Jesus was talking about loosing something on the earth because the money you need is already in the earthly realm although it might be in possession of wicked people. Therefore, when you release it using your Heavenly authority, it is loosed from the hands of the wicked and start to gravitate like a current, streaming in your direction. Owing to lack of revelation, some people think that when you loose money on the earth, the Lord looses money in Heaven. But, no, the Lord in Heaven looses the money which is here on the earth. The Lord is saying, "When you loose money, using your authority on the earth, I will loose the ability to cause that which you said to come to pass." It's as if the Lord is also saying, "Whatsoever you *don't* bind on the earth shall *not* be bound in Heaven. And whatsoever you *don't* loose on earth shall *not* be loosed in Heaven." In other words, He's saying, "I can't permit it unless you permit it." So we know that if *we* permit money to come to us—if we loose it—*God* will permit it to come to us. He will loose it and when God looses something, it is loosed.

> *Poverty, lack, debt, discontentment or discouragement cannot hold us anymore, because we can exercise our covenant rights to prosper and be elevated to the realm of millionaires.*

To cement this divine revelation with further scriptural evidence, the Bible records in Mathew 13:17-2, an incident whereby Jesus loosed a woman whose back had been bunt over for over eighteen years. According to the narrative, Jesus commanded, *"Woman thou art loosed from thine infirmity"*, and she was instantly loosed. Do you notice that when Jesus loosed the woman from the bondage, results were instantaneous? There was no procrastination due to unwavering faith. This is the same principle by which Miracle money is demonstrated. When you command it to appear in the natural realm, you must not expect it to appear after hours of prayer but immediately after you command it into manifestation. One striking reality is that according to Jesus, this woman was a daughter of Abraham who had a covenant of healing. Just as it was that woman's right to be loosed from her infirmity, it is *our* right to be loosed from poverty, lack and debt. Christ has redeemed us from the curse of the Law. He has *loosed* us from the curse of the Law. *Poverty* is a curse just as *sickness* is a curse. And *prosperity* is a blessing just as *healing* is a blessing. Just as we have been legally loosed from poverty, we can make certain demands on our covenant and command prosperity—and that includes Miracle money—to come our way. When we say, *"Money, thou art loosed!"* we are boldly testifying and witnessing to the fact that debt, discontentment, discouragement, and lack cannot hold us anymore, because we know our covenant rights and we are using our mouth, not just in words but in power and in much assurance of faith, to appropriate the money we need in the natural realm.

It must therefore be ingrained in your thinking that every time you use the term, *"Money, thou art loosed!"* you'll see with the eyes of faith, Miracle money raining down upon you because you've taken authority over money. You see, you have to *command* money to come to you. You have to make demands on money. The greater truth is that you can't just *wish* it would come; that will never work. You have to use the same authority Jesus used when He said to that woman, *"Woman, thou art loosed from thine infirmity."* In Luke 13, even though Jesus was talking about this woman's healing in connection with the covenant, we know we can apply what He said to other areas, too, such as finances, because our covenant includes more than healing. I want you to understand that if you take your place in Christ and do the things God wants you to do concerning money, it has no other choice except to obey you. It has to be loosed if you command it to. However, you must understand that in some instances, Miracle money might not manifest itself in a direct financial form but indirectly through the deposit of air time into people's cell phones, resuscitation of old equipment, electric gargets or cars without having a mechanic to fix them as well as driving cars without spending money on fuel. During ministerial sessions, the power of God can go beyond the church walls such that it touches and resuscitates malfunctioning possessions of congregates such as cars, electric gargets, animals, pets and anything that belongs to them even in their absence. This is an indirect manifestation of Miracle money because the money that believers could have used to repair these gargets is now used to advance the gospel.

The greater truth is that the key to provoking an avalanche of Miracle money is worship. A heightened degree of Praise and worship can break the chains of financial bondage of poverty, lack or debt and launch us into the depths of financial prosperity and catapult us into the realm of millionaires. To cement this revelation with scriptural evidence, the Bible further records an incident in Acts 16 whereby Paul and Silas had been beaten and thrown in prison for preaching the Gospel: *"And when they had laid many stripes upon them, they cast them into prison, charging the jailer to keep them safely, Who, having received such a charge, thrust them into the inner prison, and made their feet fast in the stocks. And at midnight Paul and Silas prayed, and sang praises unto God: and the prisoners heard them. And suddenly there was a great earthquake, so that the foundations of the prison were shaken: and immediately all the doors were opened, and every one's bands were loosed.*" There is a great revelation gleaned in this narrative. Some people have been experiencing "midnight" in their finances, but Jesus have come to bring them daylight. Do you know what I mean by *"midnight"*? I mean, it's dark in the arena of your finances. You love God, attend church and walk in love toward others yet it's dark in your finances. You need an opening somewhere for light to come in on your situation. Miracle money is the solution to that darkness in the arena of finances, which is a product of praise and worship. That's what can happen for you, too, when you pray and sing praises to God. Notice something else about that verse. It says, *"... Suddenly there was a great earthquake and immediately all the doors were opened, and every one's bands were loosed."* God knows how to turn things around for you *suddenly* and cause things to *immediately* become better for you! By the same token, in your finances, you could read that verse this way: *"Suddenly, there was a great earthquake, so that the foundations of debt, distress, discontentment, lack, and poverty were shaken: and immediately all the doors were opened, and everyone's bands were loosed."* God wants to shake the foundation of your money problem and open doors of opportunity for you to have plenty! There's no lock strong enough to lock what Jesus has loosed! There's no rope or chain strong enough to hold back what He's loosed. I tell you, the devil does not have a big enough rope to hold you back and keep you broke!

Moreover, the Bible gives an account of Lazarus in John 11:14 who had died and was four days buried in the grave until Jesus stepped on the scene and turned around the situation. When Jesus came, He commanded, "Lazarus, come forth!" Then notice what happened: *And he that was dead came forth, bound hand and foot with grave clothes: and his face was bound about with a napkin. Jesus said unto them, loose him, and let him go.* Note that Lazarus had been in the grave for four days. His sister Martha said to Jesus, "Lord, he stinks by now", but that didn't stop Jesus. In the context of this revelation, our "dead," stinky financial condition is not going to stop Him, either! Jesus has already called us to come forth. When He redeemed us by fulfilling God's great plan of redemption, He called us forth out of darkness and into His light. He called us forth out of poverty and into His riches. But many of us are still bound. We still have on those old grave clothes with that napkin on our face where prosperity is concerned. We haven't seen the truth as we ought. We haven't been able to walk in the light of prosperity as we ought. The way we're going to get ourselves untied and get our money untied is by taking hold of the truth by faith and by *commanding* money to be loosed unto us. We can't "try it and see if it works." And we can't wish money were loosed unto us. No, we have to say, *"Money, thou art loosed!"* and witness a torrential down pour of Miracle money flooding every area where there is lack and insufficiency in our lives, glory to Jesus!

CHAPTER SEVEN

SPIRITUAL LAWS GOVERNING THE OPERATION AND MANIFESTATIONS OF ANGELS

It is essential for us to know how to be in a prime position to receive and activate God's supernatural influence of angels in our world. One of the main things we need to understand is how the kingdom of God works in relation to us and our earthly realm. There are certain kingdom laws in the Word of God that angels abide by, and if we are to benefit from having angels as our allies, we too must abide by those laws. We need to understand that angels are real beings and they have laws by which they are governed and which they function in. Some of the laws are initiated from God's side while some are on our side. God operates under a set of strict spiritual laws that I would say most Christians do not understand. God created natural things as patterns for things that are found in the spiritual realm. Just as there are natural and physical laws that rule and control our outcomes, there are also spiritual laws that control our eternal destiny. God is a highly organized being of supreme intelligence, hence He put in place structures and laws to govern His spiritual Kingdom. These laws govern and control what you get out of life. God gives us great information about these laws in the Bible so that we can learn to use them to help us to live life to the fullest. God gives us a number of great examples in the Bible of people utilizing these laws to achieve great things. God also gives us examples of people who did not follow these spiritual laws and how they came to a less than admirable ending. By cooperating with the spiritual laws we are far less likely to fall into calamity.

These laws affects what we do and the results that we have regardless of whether we are thinking of them or not. A law whether natural or spiritual is no respecter of person. If you don't understand the law of gravity you will still die if you jump off a cliff. We have to respect those laws God made in the spirit world. The laws of motion, the laws of gravity, the laws of thermodynamics and the laws of aerodynamics are just a few of these scientific systems that we depend upon. God created these natural systems so that we could depend upon and have confidence in them every day by faith. You may or may not understand how these laws work, but yet you can believe in them and use them to your advantage or your harm depending on what you desire to happen. For example, if you want to go to California from New York, the law of aerodynamics can help your pilot override the laws of gravity and help you to get you there in a matter of a couple of hours or so by plane. This is just a small example of how natural laws help us in our everyday lives.

67. *The law of attraction*

To better understand the Law of Attraction, see yourself as a magnet attracting unto you the essence of that which you are thinking and feeling. If you are feeling poor, you cannot attract prosperity. It defies Law. The more you come to understand the power of the Law of Attraction, the more interest you will have in deliberately directing your thoughts—for you get what you think about, whether you want it or not. Without exception, that which you give thought to is that which you begin to invite into your experience. Your body is a mirror of your deep, often unconscious, inner feelings. This law applies to the physical body. Inner feelings are reflected in the way we build our bodies. You unconsciously transmit your energy out to the Universe. Some of your qualities are magnetic and others repellent. You have drawn towards yourself everyone and everything that is in your life. In regards to the people in our lives, we attract these which represent something about ourselves, be it good or bad, positive or negative. People who do not resonate with our energetic frequency are not attracted to us. The same goes for angels. If you don't think about angels manifesting in your life, you might not attract the angelic grace.

Spiritual Laws & Principles of The Kingdom

The vibration you emit is made up of your conscious and unconscious energy – some repellent, some magnetic, some neutral. The underlying law is 'like attracts like'. We attract into our lives people and situations that have similar vibrations to our own. Negative qualities such as depression, neediness, selfishness, desperation, greediness, unkindness or thoughtlessness transmit on a low frequency. If we have these elements in our personalities we will magnetize someone with similar energy into your life. Positive qualities such as love, happiness, kindness, delight and generosity transmit on a higher frequency energy and magnetizes people with similar energy into your life. Our underlying beliefs attract situations and people to us. If you have a belief that you are not deserving, you will attract people into your life who mirror that belief back to you by treating you badly. The same goes for angelic manifestation. If you constantly preoccupy your thoughts about angels, they will automatically manifest as you release divine energy that draws them to you.

The Law of Attraction works on many levels. If you are out of harmony with life you may attract food which disagrees with you. If you think self-critical thoughts then you are taking little swipes at yourself. If you are burying rage you may draw in attack. If you feel you do things because you feel you 'should' or feel obligated, then you are in bondage. You will attract situations and people that keep you bound. If you think negative thoughts you will attract negative people and situations. If you are sending out positive energy, you will attract help when you need it. The inner attracts the outer. If something in your outer world is not what you want it to be, look inside and shift how you feel about yourself. You will then automatically attract different people and experiences to you. Do not send out negative energy and wait for a disaster to be magnetized towards you. Send out positive energy and wait for a miracle to be drawn towards you. Do you remember that God caused the quails to be drawn in the direction of the children of Israel so that they can eat meat? This is the basis of the law of attraction. It is apparent that the quails were attracted to God's agenda; that's why they streamed in the direction of the children of Israel. In a similar fashion, where there is need for God's purpose to be fulfilled in your life, God will draw angels in your direction so that they can assist you tin fulfilling that purpose.

68. *The law of attention*

The law of attention stipulates that whatever you focus on and give your attention to, will manifest. "Energy flows where attention goes". This spiritual law ensures that an outcome manifests to the exact percentage you give it your attention. Attention is the focus of your thoughts, words and actions.

Lives differ according to the expectations of the individual. People who are in similar life situations will each hold a different picture of the expected outcome. Accordingly, each will create a slightly different result, as each person creates their own reality. The only thing that stops you from manifesting your dreams, goals and desires, is your own doubts and fears. Watch where you put your thoughts. As we travel the road of life we are asked to pay attention to signs and symbols the Universe presents to guide us along our way. If you give attention to a fear or worry, you energize it and bring it into creation. Picturing worse-case scenarios in your mind, or continually talking to others about your fears, are powerful ways of drawing that fear into your life. Remember, the positive has a more powerful charge than the negative. When you hold the positive in your attention, you make your dreams, goals and desires come to fruition. When you hold the vision and do the necessary work, success is assured. Focus on what you want and you will get it. 'Be careful what you wish for as you just might get it.' The same goes with angelic manifestation. If angels' attempts to manifest themselves and someone you are too busy to pay attention or rather insensitive to their visitation, they might end up not manifesting themselves to you. I believe the reason why the angel of the Lord called Moses in the bush is because he paid attention and drew closer to see why there was fire in the bush yet it was not burnt. The more he paid attention and focused on the angelic scene, the more the angel spoke to him. That is why I hinted earlier that "Energy flows where attention goes".

69. *The law of manifestation*

The law of manifestation stipulates that the extent to which anything whether blessing, breakthrough or angels can manifest in your life is grossly dependent on your ability to make it manifest. Everything in the Universe has an energetic frequency of its own, and it is broadcasting on the etheric level. Your task is to tune-in to the vibrational frequency of the vision you seek. This will access the information you need to draw it into your life. Your constant thoughts send out interference which stops you from fine-tuning to the frequency you need to be able to draw it in. Be certain you know exactly what you want, otherwise you may receive something other than what you wished for. Clarity is the key to manifestation. Be still, clear and precise. If you want to attract a friend who is open-hearted, fun-loving and light, then you must develop those desired qualities in yourself. The ability to manifest is extremely powerful so it is important that you manifest only for the highest good. As soon as you have clarity, clearly picture what you want.

Visualization is an important element in the manifestation of angels. You must have absolute faith that your intention will come to fruition. If you have difficulty with gaining clarity, write down exactly what you want. If you want for a partner, write down exactly what qualities you would like them to have and remember to have those same qualities in return within yourself. If you wish to manifest a car, write down exactly what you need. Picture it, visualize it, and then make sure you are sending out the right vibrations that match the vibration of the car. Focus on the higher qualities of that which you are manifesting. The same goes for angels. When angels operate on the earth, they are not earthly or fleshly beings but spiritual beings who operate in the spirit realm. Therefore in order to ensure greater cooperation with them, you needs to be move in the dimension of the spirit. It does not necessarily mean that angels should manifest themselves in a visible form in order for us to know that there are present. Make an effort to use your imagination to visualise angelic presence, then make sure you are sending out the right vibrations that match the vibration of angelic manifestation. Before long, you will witness angels manifesting in your life like never before.

70. *The Law of Release*

It is important to understand that angels needs to be released in order for them to work in our behalf. The law of release is such a powerful divine prophetic principle which when tapped into, can result in an avalanche of God's anointing that carries angels from the realm of the spirit into visible manifestation in the natural realm. Do you remember when God declared in Zechariah 10:1 that, *"Ask for rain in the time of the latter rain and I shall give you showers of abundant rain"*? This is the essence of the *law of release*. Rain speaks of the anointing and in the context of supernatural power, this implies that if you need an unprecedented flow or avalanche of God's anointing, you must release it during the right time when the power of God is moving or flowing. This spiritual law awakens us to the consciousness that it is advisable to release angels when people are ready to receive or when the spiritual atmosphere is conducive enough to unleash or release the power of God. Hence, there are two critical prerequisites for the release of God's angels and that is; the extent to which the atmosphere and spiritual climate is pregnant with the possibilities of God and the extent to which people are ready to receive from God. The Bible further declares in Ecclesiastics 11:3 that *when clouds are full of rain, they empty themselves on earth*. Knowing when to release the power is one such a vital key to the flow of God's angels. That is why Paul advises in 1 Timothy 5:22 that *no one must not be quick to lay hands* because at times the anointing might be building up like a cloud or accumulating until a particular point. Making haste to release the power under such circumstances might not produce expected results. The expectancy level of people somehow is a determining factor to the law of release. You only release the power when your faith level and expectancy levels of people are high.

This implies that we cannot declare the word if we don't have foreknowledge of what will happen. For example, if you are going to speak to a blind person yet you don't expect his sight to return, then rather don't say anything and if you are going to tell the lame to stand up yet you don't expect anything to happen, you rather not say anything at all. Apostolic revelation breaks new ground by declaring what the father is saying and doing at this moment in time. This causes the Heavens to loose what God has authorised for the earth. When the Holy Spirit reveals something through the apostles and prophets, Heaven can no longer contain it, it must be released. However, the greatest challenge facing the Body of Christ is that Heavens are pregnant with the possibilities of God and is therefore ready to unleash from the womb of the Spirit the power, anointing and glory but the earth is not ready to receive or incubate that which Heaven has given birth to in the spirit realm. That is why in some cases, there is so much power that is released from Heaven but it never gets to be utilised effectively because people are not sensitive to the move of God. This is contrary to the will of God because Jesus declared in Mathew 18:18 that, *"Whatever we bind on earth shall be bound in heaven and whatever we release on earth shall be released in Heaven"* This means as far as God is concerned, Heaven and earth are supposed to function in synchronisation, in order to release the blessings of God. It is God's ultimate plan that Heaven and earth work together as one and not as separate entities. If you understand the law of release, you will know when to ask and when your blessing has arrived after praying for it. The danger is that so many believers are praying and praying but they never get to know when their prayers have been answered or when their blessings have been released. The truth is that *release* and *reception* takes place concurrently. In other words, blessings are received from Heaven the instant they are released into the natural realm. Contrary to how the lukewarm church has portrayed, you don't release the blessings or power of God today and then wait for tomorrow in order to see the results. Instead, you must procure the blessings at that very time when you release them. With this understanding, you certainly realise that blessings manifests at the point of release, hence there is no need for waiting and procrastination.

Spiritual Laws & Principles of The Kingdom

71. *The Law of Response*

The law of response is such a powerful divine principle that precedes the law of release because in prophetic language, you can only respond to something that has been released. Do you remember when God declared in Jeremiah 33:3 that, *"Call unto me and I will answer thee and show you great and mighty things which you knewest not"*. This is the essence of the *law of response*. This law gives a practical guide on how to respond to the anointing, presence and angels of God when administered from Heaven. It states that in order to activate or harness God's power from the supernatural realm and precipitates it into the natural realm; you must be in a position to respond accordingly when you sense its presence in the atmosphere. In other words, your spirit must be in an upper room position to respond to what God is appropriating in the spirit realm. Whenever the presence of God shows up, there are always three types of people who would usually respond in a particular way under normal circumstances. Firstly, there are those who are *spectators*, and have no clue of what God is doing in the spirit realm, hence they don't take any notice of His presence. Secondly, there are those who are *resistors* and are able to sense the presence of God but they are simply resisting it because their spirit is closed. Thirdly, there are those who are *detectors* and are able to feel the presence and desire to participate in it but have no revelation of how to channel the presence or benefit from it. The word of God gives an account in Luke 5:17 of how *the power of the Lord was present to heal*. In other words, the atmosphere was charged with God's presence but nothing happened until four men took a leap of faith and lowered a bedridden man through the roof and he was the first to receive his healing. However, there are those who are *partakers,* who have received a revelation of how to respond quickly whenever they sense the presence of God. And notable is the realisation that it is this last group that always excels in matters of demonstrating the power of God. This is akin to the incident in Mark 9:20, whereby people were pressing upon Jesus but only one woman who had a flow of blood for twelve years knew the art of how to respond to the anointing and sneaked her way through to touch the hem of Jesus' garment and she instantly received her healing.

It is a typical scenario in many churches that God's presence is felt but nothing more happens. His presence is there because some people paid a price for it but now that it comes,   no one knows precisely how to respond or how to act whenever confronted by the presence.   The atmosphere remains charged yet no one actively participates in it. This culminates in a scenario whereby miracles, signs and wonders and transformations are delayed because people have no idea of how to respond and appropriate the blessings of God. It is wrong to find some people being spectators in the presence of God because God demands that he who comes in His presence must participate in order to reap benefits of power and blessings from it. The power of God meets every need depending on individual desire and while others are receiving deliverance, others are being healed and others receive breakthroughs and impartation of spiritual substances. Hence, the correct prayer that we should pray whenever the presence of God shows up is *"Lord, reveal the purpose of your presence"*. This is because whenever God show up, He comes for a specific purpose and what He wants to do today might be different from what He did yesterday. We therefore need to respond to the angels of God through elevated worship, prophetic declaration and proclamation of our blessings, shouting for victory, dancing and yelling in praise as well as through practical demonstration and exercise of the gifts of the spirit.

72. *The Law of expectation*

The expectancy level is such a powerful key that can provoke the angels of God into manifestation. The Bible says in Acts 3:5, that when Peter and John came across a crippled man at the Beautiful gate of the temple, he gave them attention expecting to receive something and that is the reason why he received his healing on that day. In fact, every day, they had passed by that man on their way to the temple and this was not the first time. But on that day, the man was in a better position to believe. Sometimes, when you remain in an atmosphere of faith, your faith grows until you are expectant enough to receive. Likewise, on that day he passed by the Beautiful gate, Peter sensed that the man was expectant and rightly positioned in the spirit to receive, hence he healed him. The truth is that regardless of the level of anointing upon a vessel, no one can give you what you are not ready to receive. As a believer, you must expect to receive a miracle whenever you get to a place where the presence of God is moving. Unfortunately, there are certain preachers who struggle to help even their own congregation because they themselves lack genuine expectancy. A high level of expectancy places a demand on the anointing and produces tremendous angelic manifestation. Miracles tend to intensify when the expectancy level is high. The law of expectation is such a powerful divine principle in that miracles do not happen where they are needed but they occur where they are expected. The higher the level of expectation, the greater the dimension of miracles, signs and wonders and the greater the manifestation of angels.

There is however an intricate connection between *expectancy level* and the *law of response*. For example, to respond to the angels of God, we need to expect something supernatural to happen. If we do not expect anything, then we will be unable to respond when there is a manifestation of angels. God is extending His hand to give us the supernatural but we also have to extend our hands in return to receive it. The reason why God demands in Exodus 23:15 that *no man should come into His presence empty handed* is because He knows that if you come empty handed, you will not expect to receive anything from Him, hence He challenges you to bring something so as to stir up your faith level. In a ministerial context, as you minister, you must watch the response of the people because how the congregation responds is vital for the smooth flow of God's power. Stirring up their readiness can be done in different ways, for example by declaring *"Are you ready for the angels of the God?"* How they respond will tell you whether they are really ready and rightly positioned in the sprit to receive or not. Keep declaring that angels are around and ministering to the congregation. As you declare these words, the expectancy level will provoke faith in their spirits such that some will even begin to see angels. This is the power behind the *law of expectation*.

73. *The law of expression*

Knowing how to express your spirit in God's presence without shame, fear, hesitation or unbelief is such a key determinant to partaking of angelic presence. Expression in this regard entails developing a high level of *sensitivity, acknowledgment and consciousness of God's angels*. Some people are not able to see angels because they are not *sensitive* to the move of the spirit. In other words, they cannot sense or detect their presence due to the fact their spiritual senses have not yet been activated, developed or trained to operate in the spirit realm. Moreover, some people do not receive because they are not *conscious* or cannot discern God's angels. Developing one's level of consciousness through spending time in the presence of God is one such vital key to receiving or flowing in the angelic realm. *Acknowledgment* of the angels of God present is also a highly imperative action.

The Bible records in Mathew 20:29-34, that *when the blind man heard that Jesus was passing by, he cried out loud* and because of his high level of expression, Jesus healed him. According to the culture of the people at that time, it was a taboo for a man in his sins to cry out to a Rabai but because of his desire to reach out to God, the man expressed himself vocally until Jesus paid attention to his cry and healed him. The scripture further proclaims in Genesis 18:1, that *when Abraham saw three angels purporting to be passing by, he ran after them and invited them to come to his house* and because of his expression, he was blessed at the end. All these are physical expressions but there are also different ways of expressing one's self in the spirit and that is through praying in other tongues, laughing and singing in the spirit, dancing in the spirit, travailing in prayer, falling under the power. By the same token, how one expresses himself will determine the degree of angelic manifestation.

It is evident that other people try to resist or stop the flow of spiritual expressions and in the process they short circuit or deactivate the power of God. For example, the Bible records a myriad of incidents where men of God expressed themselves fully before God. For instance, David danced in the presence of the Lord until his clothes were torn, the apostles were so drunk in the spirit on the day of Pentecost to the extent that they were out of control, Saul prophesied until he tore his clothes off although this manifestation ended up being in the flesh. These were such powerful expressions that launched them into greater depths in the spirit. However, while in the presence of God, some people tend to maintain their cool and be overly conscious of their self and in the process they fail to express themselves, hence receive nothing from God. It is therefore advisable that you release yourself unreservedly in the presence of God because the extent to which your spirit is open will determine the degree of angelic manifestation.

74. *The Law of Connection*

It is a greater truth that angelic manifestation flows through divine connection. Jesus declared in John 15:13-17 that, "*I am the vine and you are the braches grafted in the vive, therefore abide in me and I shall abide in you.* This implies that if you stay connected to God, His divine power will continuously flow upon your life and the opposite is true. Do you know that when the Bible says in Psalms 91:1 that *He that dwells in the secret place shall abide by the shadow of the almighty*, it actually speak of divine connection? This fruits or results of such divine connection are protection, prosperity, promotion, increase and so forth. Therefore, continuously staying in the presence of God will also ensure that you manifest angels greatly. However, angels' do not only flow when you are connected to God but when you are connected to those upon whom the Lord has made an investment of His power. Our ability to manifest angels is closely related with those to whom God has connected you. God will connect you to specific people, hence we must be a wise discerner of relationships. It is through relationships that we capture the mantles and blessings upon those whom God has connected us. On the other hand, if you disconnect yourself from a spiritual covering, you lose the anointing because one would have been cut off from the atmosphere, association and influence, in the same way a branch is cut off from a tree. However, some divine relationships are under heavy attack because whenever God connects us to someone, Satan will try to destroy the relationship because he knows that if we never make such a connection, our purpose will never be completed. Therefore, if you want to launch into greater depths of angelic manifestation, connect yourself to a man of God who has the angelic grace and angels will stream in your direction.

The law of connection also implies being at the right place, at the right time, doing the right thing. The law of connection entails connecting yourself to two fundamental sources of power, that is, *connection to God* and *connection to His word*. Connecting one's self to the word of God is tantamount to connecting yourself to God because He has placed His word above His name. Hence, you are guaranteed of *kratos power* that is leased from the pages of the Bible straight into your spirit when you meditate on the word of God. That *kratos* power will in turn provoke angelic manifestation. Do you remember that the Bible declares in Psalms 1:1-6, that *blessed is a man who walks not in the counsel of the ungodly, nor stand in the seat of the scornful but his delight is in the law of the Lord and upon it he meditates day and night. He shall be like a tree planted by many rivers, whatever he does prospers.* Do you notice that prosperity is conditional; in other words it is dependent on the extent to which you mediate on the word of God? By the same token angelic manifestation is conditional; it is dependent on the extent to which you are connected to the angelic grace or covering. This is the essence of *connection*. The above scripture unveils the reality that angelic manifestation depends on the extent to which one is connected to the word of God.

75. *The Law of Contagious Experience*

The law of contagious experience states that whenever the angels of God are moving and everyone is connected in the spirit, if one person catches the angelic manifestations, the rest will catch it too. Do you know that if one person raises the dead in your church, other members and churches in the neighbourhood will catch it too such that within a twinkling of an eye, the whole city will be in a Holy Ghost flame. By the same token, if one begins to see angels constantly, others might end up experiencing the same angelic manifestations too. The manifestations of the spirit are contagious in the sense that they are easily transmitted to other people. Some manifestations are common or popular amongst certain ministries as a result of the application of the law of contagious experience. There is a spiritual law in principle that we don't really know anything until we have experienced it. You can know something through somebody else's sharing or through reading the Word of God but we do not really know the matter until we have experienced it. God is a person and He wants us to experience Him as a person. For example, your relationship with your wife is a legal relationship but at the same time, it is a personal relationship. A house is a house but the relationships within the house make it a home. Christianity is a true-life relationship with God. When you experience God, you experience Him in the spiritual world, which has a side effect on our soul and on our body. Likewise, we can never really understand working with angels until we have had a spiritual contact and experience with them. However, we cannot base theology on experience. Theology must be based on the Word of God. But the experience helps us to look at the Word in a different way. Without the experience, I believe none of us will look at the Word in a different way.

If one person sees angels, other people will start seeing angels. It becomes an angel's meeting. Who knows a new revival of seeing angels? Remember the law of contagious. It is caught, more than taught. That also gives you a safety valve. If you do not feel comfortable with the manifestation, you do not want it. Just do not hang around. Remember, experience can be caught. For example, if you have an anointing upon your life and when you associate with different people, the same gifting will start operating through some of these people. It is a law of association. In this teaching, I put it as a law of contagious experience and we need to understand that law is working all the time. It can be working positively or negatively. Nevertheless, when something is going on and you need to be touched, you need to have the experience, hang around that group. Hang around people with that experience, it will rub off you. If in your life, you want to experience the word of knowledge frequently or discerning of spirits or a vision in God, hang around people who do. It will rub on you. This is the law of contagious experiences and that law is operating all the time. On the positive side if you do not have that experience and you know that experience is good for you, hang around with people with that kind of experience. Join them; be next to them in the prayer meeting.

In I Sam., when he was first anointed in 1 Samuel 10:10-11, When he came to there to the hill, there was a group of prophets to meet him; then the Spirit of God came upon him and he prophesied among them. And it happened, when all who knew him formerly saw that he indeed prophesied among the prophets, that the people said to one another, "What is this that has come upon the son of Kish? Is Saul also among the prophets?" Now again those soldiers he sent to catch David, they were not prophets but they came into the atmosphere of people prophesying. I do not know what it was like but I could imagine some of them were playing the timbre and harp when the soldiers came looking for David. They were not enrolled in the school of prophets. They were those with swords in their hands looking for David. When they came, they heard the prophets prophesying and they too began to prophesy. Again, the law of contagious experience and then they go into a place where people gather and the anointing soaks into the place. The Presence of God was still very strong in that place but what Saul did was not right. The Spirit was right. The experience was right. Even the prophecy was of God but what he did was in the flesh. That is just an example to show that when the Spirit of God moves it does not mean that all the experiences can be of God. However, not all manifestation needs to be of God because all of us have different soul needs.

76. *The Law of Association*

It is an undeniable fact that angels of God manifests greatly through association or relationships hence Paul declared in 1 Corinthians 11:1 that *imitate me as I imitate Jesus*. Through this principle, power was able to flow from Paul to the churches. As they emulated him, they were thrust into the same degree of power at which he was operating. The Bible says, *"Now when they saw the boldness of Peter and John, and perceived that they were unlearned and ignorant men, they marvelled; and they took knowledge of them, that they <u>had been with Jesus</u>"* (Acts 4.13). In the context of this scripture, the phrase, *"had been with Jesus"* speaks of the *law of association*. In other words, it is because of their association with Jesus that people took heed of their message. Moreover, the Bible says *Joshua son of Nun was full of the spirit of wisdom; for Moses had laid his hands upon him: and the children of Israel hearkened unto him, and did as the LORD commanded Moses"* (Deuteronomy 34:9). This implies that it was because of his association with Moses that the people hearkened to the voice of Joshua. Every time they looked at Joshua, they saw Moses in him. This is just how powerful the law of contagious association is. Moreover, Elisha received the mantle by virtue of association with Elijah. If it wasn't for association, I don't believe he would have received even the *double portion* from him. He followed Elijah closely as he ate from his hand until the reward time came and Elisha scooped the spoils.

It is a divine truth that in order to move in greater dimensions of angelic manifestation, you need to be part of people or church that moves in that grace. Corporate anointing comes through the law of association. It is for this reason that Paul warned believers in Hebrews 10:25 *not to neglect the gathering of saints*. David further describes how pleasant it is for brethren to fellowship or associate together. As you enter into the season of the supernatural, God will cause your relationships to change because one key to becoming a carrier of God's power is not to be emotionally tied to people who are potential obstacles to your receiving and flowing in the power especially if those people have a traditional, denominational and rigid mentality that keeps them from changing for the better. By virtue of association, even the blessings of God can spill over to touch those close to you in your sphere of contact in the same way Lot got blessed by virtue of his association with Abraham and Laban got blessed because of Jacob (Genesis 30:25-43).

77. *The law of atmosphere*

A conducive atmosphere, ambiance and spiritual climate must be fostered in an endeavour to trigger the flow of God's angels in a specific territory. God has always been known to speak from the cloud of His glory, hence it is important to know how to build a spiritual atmosphere. The spiritual atmosphere is the cloud of God's presence that surrounds us. We must therefore create a celestial atmosphere for angelic manifestation through the word we speak. When you get to a level where your faith cannot operate, change the atmosphere. Unfortunately, many people are in places where angelic manifestation is non-existent because a divine atmosphere was never generated. The atmosphere is generated through a myriad of spiritual exercises such as praise and worship, prayer and intercession which build the tabernacle where God's glory can manifest. After man was disconnected from the glory of God as a result of sin, the only way to bring it back was through praise and worship. However, the duration of praise and worship depends on the extent to which the environment or atmosphere is cultivated. If the atmosphere is hard to pierce, it will take longer to build the throne but where an atmosphere already exists, one can go directly into worship. Moreover, it is also important to discern the atmosphere whether it is for miracles, healing, deliverance or angelic manifestation after that speak into that atmosphere in order to make what you declare come to pass. In Genesis 1:1-10, when God spoke and said *let there be light*, the Holy Spirit who had already created a conducive atmosphere by brooding over the face of the deep, acted on the word which God spoke and brought those things which God spoke into manifestation. This is the same principle by which we operate in the angelic realm whenever we want to provoke a greater manifestation of angels.

78. *The law of confession*

The first law of operating in the angelic realm is to understand the power of words. Words are the capsules that contain the believer's anointing and release it forth. Angelic manifestation depends on the word we speak. The next time you want to release God's angels, speak it out verbally. You know you are releasing tremendous authority and power over substances that you partake of. The law of confession is one of the most powerful ways in which you can be instantly catapulted into the realm of God's power. By definition, *"confession"* refers to the prophetic declaration, proclamation, pronunciation and utterance of God's word with a view to effecting changes in our situations and circumstances by the use of our tongue. In a practical sense, it means speaking forth the word of God from the depths of our spirits with the intent to change the prevailing situation and circumstances and to produce the results the word of God talks about. The word *"confession"* comes from the Greek word homologous, which means confessing the word of God. The word *homo* means same and *logos* means the word of God. *Homologous* therefore means confessing with the words of our mouth or saying exactly the same words that God says. The Bible declares in Proverbs 18:21 that death and life are in the power of the tongue. This means that confession is a powerful creative force, which can catapult a man to the highest realms and dimensions of power.

Therefore, since you can only receive what you confess in the angelic realm, talking is very important because your words will reap a harvest. Philosophically speaking, your mouth rules in the realm of God's power, since the demonstration of power depends on what you say. Words were not made primarily for communication purposes; that is secondary. Instead, words were given specifically to release creative power in your spirit. In essence, words are God's method of operation by which He accomplishes His will, purpose and desire. There are pipelines for divine exploits. Words set spiritual laws in motion. Words are spiritual containers that carry power. Words are seeds sown with your mouth that produce their own kind. Words are the process starters of life. Words are the building blocks with which you construct your life and future. Words set the cornerstones of your life. Words program the human spirit for exploits. Words have creative ability. They create the realities you see. God's word—the incorruptible seed – has within it the ability and DNA to cause itself to come to pass. This means that God's word has potency to produce what it talks about. Just by speaking God's word alone is enough to turn around the situation. In Luke 7:6-7, the centurion pleaded with Jesus saying, *"I do not even think of myself worthy to come to you but say the word and my servant will be healed"*. Note that the centurion wasn't asking Jesus to say just anything; instead he was asking Him to speak God's word to turn around his situation. In today; language what the centurion was saying is, *"Lord, your word is just enough to change my situation"* and because He took God at His word, he was labelled as the one with the greatest faith in Israel simply because he believed in confessing God's word. Faith could therefore be best described as speaking God's word with intent to change situations and circumstances.

To cement this revelation with reference to scriptural evidence, Jesus declared in Mark 11:23, *"If you say to a mountain be thou removed and be cast into the sea and you do not doubt but believe that those things which you say shall come to pass, then you shall have whatever you say."* This implies that if you don't say it, then you cannot have it. If you can't confess that you are functioning in the angelic realm, then you cannot expect to see angels. If you do not confess angels, you cannot see angels. Words establish strongholds, break habits, change things and redirect thought patterns. Words point you in whatever direction they are aimed and released. Words set the course of your life. Words determine your future, your health, your wealth and your place in eternity. Words arrive at your future before you do. Words create desires and transmit images that you will eventually live out. Words frame your world. Words spoken today become a living reality tomorrow. Words give permission and licence to spiritual forces to work for you or against you. Words make demands on the blessing or the curse—whichever you call for. Words are goal setters that give direction and establish destination. Words are our method of operation, by which God accomplishes His will, purpose and desire for our lives. Words can turn around any situation. As a matter of fact, there is nothing on this earth so great or so powerful, including the physical body, which cannot be turned around by our words. Even death can be reversed by words; that is why the Bible says *death and life are in the power of the tongue.* The entire course of nature and the circumstances surrounding every human being are controlled by that person's words. We don't have a choice whether or not we live by words. We do, however, have a choice of what words we live by. If your mouth will feed your heart the word of faith when you don't need it—your heart will feed your mouth the word of faith when you do need it. We appropriate what is ours in Christ by making God's word a daily part of our vocabulary. We are to confess what we can do in Christ, who we are in Christ and what we have in Christ.

79. *The Law of desire*

It must be understood that according to this spiritual law, spiritual things including angelic manifestations are granted through desire. Those who genuinely desire God's supernatural angelic manifestations are the best candidates for receiving it. In the natural realm if we feel hunger, we tend to forget the norms of courtesy because we seek only to satisfy our yearnings. The same happens in the angelic realm. Only those who hunger or thirst for angelic manifestation in their lives are the candidates to receive it. You must have a desire, passion or an inspiration to become a miracle worker for, without the desire or passion, your dream to launch the world into an arena of divine exploits, won't have a long-lasting effect. As a matter of fact, the Bible says in Psalms 37:4 that *God will grant the desires of your heart* but if you don't have any desire to move in the supernatural realm, what do you expect God to work with? Therefore, your dream has to be watered by desire, which is like fire that ignites your spirit and keeps your dream ablaze. A perennial hunger, insatiable appetite and unquenchable thirst can manifest in any individual provided he is fully aware of his personal need to receive something. In 1 Samuel 1:5, *Elkanah's wife by the name of Hannah, was so desperately in need of a baby to the extent that it absorbed her consciousness* such that when she prayed, she looked as if she was drunk. This is the extent to which a desire can overwhelm a person. You see, there is a dimension that you can reach in the spirit whereby your desire to move in God's power and raise the dead gets so ingrained in your consciousness such that even your pastor will not understand you. Jacob desired the blessing to the extent of wrestling with an angel and breaking his hip because he desperately needed a blessing from God. Unless you are desperate for the power, anointing or the miraculous, you might not fully partake of it because the realm of the miraculous is provoked by desire. The extent to which you may receive from God is determined by how hungry or thirsty you are for the miraculous. It is therefore advisable that you develop an insatiable appetite for the supernatural in order to receive angelic manifestations.

80. Law of faith

Angels operate in the invisible realm and in some cases when they manifest in the physical realm, they take up the form of ordinary people such that it is difficult for people to identify them. That is why Paul strongly warned believers not to forget to entertain strangers. The reason why they disguise themselves is because God wants man to stretch out to hum in faith. Faith is such a tremendous force that can pull down the blessings and power of God from the realm of the spirit into the natural realm. The word declares in Ephesians 1:3 that *we are blessed with all spiritual blessings in heavenly places*. But how we get them to manifest from the spirit realm into the physical is by the *law of faith*. Faith transcends both realms of existence. It is a force or invisible hand that moves in the realm of the spirit to harness God's angels and then brings them to manifestation in the natural world. Without faith it is impossible to please God. In a similar vein, without faith, it is impossible to move in the angelic realm because anything done outside the context of faith is dead. When you bring all the fullness of hope into actualising, it is the law of faith working and it brings you into the first realm, the outer court. As you begin to go faithfully into that realm, faith becomes second nature to you. Then you enter into the second realm, faith naturalised. It becomes so natural in you that you live above the law because you fulfil the law and you enter into the divine presence of His love. It is a spiritual principle that miracles exist in the now. Sadly, some preachers preach miracles in the future and speak them in a future tense saying God will heal you, God will visit us, hence by so doing they have caused miracles to be delayed. Rarely do they declare what God is doing and saying now. This is not how faith should operate. Therefore, if you want to see a greater manifestation of miracles in your life, church or ministry, simply believe God for the impossible and you will force the hand of God to move on your behalf.

It is a typical scenario that so many believers get so obsessed about confession such that they just confess and confess and yet ignore the crucial element that is responsible to make their confession work, which is *faith*. If you have confessed the word of God but you do not see any results of your confession, then know that there is a second factor that controls it. Don't forget the first part that says, *"Those who believe in My name,"* that is, your faith level. Your faith level controls the amount of believer's anointing released when you speak His word. If your faith level is small even though your words are big and loud but a lot of doubts behind your mind and in your heart, the anointing released is just a trickle. It is not the loudness of your words that determines the power content. Sometimes when you take authority, you can't help it if your voice does get higher or louder. But it is not just the loudness of the voice the demon obeys. But if you don't have faith, you tend to copy the method but not the principles, hence you are heading for disaster. If you want to copy, then copy the principles. And then if you don't have other methods go ahead and copy them but develop your own method

81. *The law of focusing*

The Bible records an incident in Exodus 3: 2 whereby the angel of the Lord appeared to Moses in a flame of fire in the bush and instantly, He turned aside from what he was doing to see this bush burning. Acknowledging the angel's presence involves giving him your full attention. Turning aside from whatever that is taking your attention and giving it your full attention. This is the essence of the spiritual *law of focusing*. Moses saw the bush burning for a long time but it's only when he came near the bush that he said, *"I must see why the bush is burning and yet it is not consumed."* See, he didn't know it was God yet. All he saw was a spectacular phenomenon. When he zoomed in on the phenomena, he received the details. And as he came near the bush, he heard the bush say, *"Moses, Moses,"* and that encounter marked the beginning of God's call for his life. You see, we have to zoom in before we get other details. When you look at something, it becomes more detailed. It's just like you could be passing a lot of scenery and you are not really paying any attention. But then when you focus on this **specific** plant and you began to see its condition, you begin to pay attention. It is the principle of *focusing*.

The truth is that when you don't put aside those things and focus on what God is bringing to your attention, you may loose it. Figuratively speaking, sometimes it's just a telephone ringing. There is no message yet, but the telephone is ringing. You got to pick it up. You got to pay attention and focus. Picking it up is like paying attention to those things. Sometimes in the spirit world you could be praying. And as you are praying, your attention is drawn towards something. Your mind and your will have a free choice. You could choose not to be drawn towards that. The bush could be burning and you could choose not to be drawn towards that, hence you may loose it. He wants you to turn aside and focus you attention on that something He has drawn you to. There is something that catches your attention first and you need to focus on this thing. You acknowledge by turning aside and paying attention to whatever is catching your mind. God gives you a free choice. If you respond then He would also respond.

The question that you are probably asking yourself is: How did Moses respond? As he drew near to the burning bush, the Lord called out from the burning bush, *"Moses, Moses."* Moses could have responded in different ways to that call. One of the possible responses is to run. To some of you as you walk by a tree and the tree calls you, you may wonder, *"Who was that?"*
You may respond differently or rush to collect a horse pipe in order to try and extinguish the burning flame. You could run away or you could find out what that voice is and what the spectacular burning bush is all about. Somehow Moses responded wisely and said, *"Here I am."* He doesn't even know who is there. But whoever that was knew him. If you happen to pass by a bush and someone calls you by name, some may think it's the devil hiding behind the bush trying to trap you. If you are in a supermarket and some stranger calls you, you don't challenge them, you respond, yet because they are invisible we don't respond the same way.

82. Law of timing

In these end time season, angels are manifesting visibly and physically in the natural realm because it is time. It must be understood that God operate sin times and season and while in the Old Testament dispensation, angels would appear here and there, in the last days an avalanche of angels shall appear everywhere as God ushers the world I to the depths of the miraculous in order to usher an avalanche of billions of souls into the kingdom. Therefore ministry angels are manifesting more in a visible and tangible way than ever before. As stipulated by His times and seasons, God does not do the same thing all the time. In order for us to be recipients of a torrential flow of His power, we therefore need to be sensitive to what He is doing at a particular time. Concerning the timing of the release of God's power on earth, God spoke through the Prophet Zechariah saying, *"Ask for me in the time of the latter rain and I will give you showers of rain."* In the context of this scripture, rain speaks of God's power or anointing. The fact that God says we should ask for rain *during the time of rain* means it's not every time that it rains. God operates in times and seasons; hence if you ask for rain at such a time when it's not the season of rain, you will not receive a positive response. It matters most when you ask for rain at the right time and God promises that when the correct timing is adhered to as per His calendar; the rain of power will come.

The law of timing implies doing the right thing at the right time. However, the truth is that at times people are doing the right thing but at the wrong time. A wrong timing might either result in a delay or procrastination of a blessing or a total failure for a blessing to be dispatched. The reason why many believers have not been able to receive their blessings despite the fact that they prayed and fasted is because of a lack of understanding of the law of timing. Unlike the sons of Issachar who had an acute understanding of times and seasons, hence knew what Israel ought to do at a particular time, many people do not understand or know God's timing yet it is such a critical determinant in matters of moving in God's power. Timing is very important when it comes to matters of the miraculous because just like the sons of Issachar, you need an acute understanding of what to do, how to do it and when to do it. For example, you need to understand how to channel the power of God in the direction of the Spirit. Wrong timing might yield wrong results.

In a ministerial context, there is a time during a meeting whereby you can sense that the *cloud* has been fully saturated. It is probably the best time to release God's angels upon the congregants. Sadly, many do not experience the spectacular display of angelic grace because they are too quick to demonstrate the power of God when the river of God's anointing is not even flowing. On the extreme end of scale, there are those who get too stuck in their own church programmes and agendas such that by the time they finish and want to move in power, the wave of glory would have sailed by, leaving only a residue of God's presence. This is to tell you that you need to be sensitive when you are ministering so that you don't just demonstrate the power of God anyhow, but wait for that moment when the atmosphere is Heavenly pregnant with the glory of God. It is at that time that you can know that even angels are ready to release the glory of God in abundance, hence you may not waste any time but release the contents of Heaven right on the scene.

83. Law of action and reaction

The law of action and reaction brings to light the fact that what we do in the spirit realm will always elicit a corresponding response in the natural and whatever we do in the natural is always preceded by a corresponding action in the Spirit. Did you know that God works by what you give Him? Likewise, angles work according to the word that you speak and if you don't say anything, they cannot produce anything for you in the spirit realm because they need your input to generate output. The greater truth is that Heaven responds by what the earth sends forth. In the natural realm, rain can only come when enough humidity has been released into the atmosphere to generate clouds. By the same token, if you need to receive anything from God or Heaven, including angelic manifestation, you must send something as an input in the form of prayers, fasting, consecration and meditation and other spiritual exercises that provokes a divine exchange of God's power. This is how a revival breaks out, to bring the earth to a perfect alignment with the Heavenly realm. When the earth is no longer working in perfect synchronisation with Heavens, it is a sign that a rival is needed. Jesus made it explicitly clear in Mathew 18:18, that *whatever we bind on earth shall be bound in heaven and whatever we loose on earth shall be loosed in heaven.* This is the basis of the principle of action and reaction. In other words, as you take a step of faith to release power in the natural realm, there is a corresponding action that authenticates your loosing from the Heavenly realm.

Action and reaction states that for every action you take in the supernatural realm, there will always be a corresponding reaction to that action in the natural realm. The Bible proclaims in Luke 6:38: *Give, and it shall be given unto you; good measure, pressed down, and shaken together, and running over, shall men give unto your bosom.* It further says: *ask and it shall be given to you, knock and the door shall be opened.* This implies that there is a response in the spirit realm to every action of faith that you take in the natural realm. Giving is a spiritual act and, as you act on it, there is a corresponding response that you receive in the natural realm in the form of blessings. That is why what we do in the realm of the spirit will always elicit a corresponding response in the natural and whatever we do in the natural is always preceded by a corresponding action in the Spirit. The law of action and reaction brings the realm of the natural and realm of the Spirit to work together. Revivals are triggered in this way. Do you know that people always react differently when the power of God is manifested? Consider how people reacted when the lightning of God's power was manifested on the way to Damascus in Acts. Some said it thundered, others said it roared and others just did not have a clue as to what exactly transpired. This reinforces the fact that for every action in the supernatural realm, there is always a corresponding reaction in the natural realm although the reaction itself might be manifested differently.

Another dimension to this divine principle is the law of *yielding*. In the spirit world, whatever you try hard to do or to get using your own effort might never materialise. The spirit world works more by yielding than by trying. Every time you try too hard, you might find it hard to infiltrate the angelic realm. It is for this reason that God spoke to Zerrubabel saying, *"it's not by might nor by power but by My spirit'*. In the spirit world, God's angels are more experienced by yielding and receiving rather than trying and grabbing. There are times when the Holy Spirit is addressing deep-seated emotional issues in the meeting even without a manifestation. If it's not God's will for us to have a specific angelic manifestation that we are all looking for on a given day, then let's not twist God's hand. Even the angelic realm does not work by trying and snatching, whiffing and huffing. Instead, it works by yielding to the ministry of angels. It must therefore be clear that we do not try to see angels. We don't even force an angelic appearance at all. Instead, just be aware of how to work with angels and be sensitive to their presence and as you grow in that knowledge and in the things of God, you will get to a level where you see angels and interact with them in the same way you engage your friends.

Apostle Frequency Revelator

THE AUTHOR'S PROFILE

Frequency Revelator is an apostle, called by God through His grace to minister the Gospel of the Lord Jesus Christ to all the nations of the world. He is a television minister, lecturer and gifted author, whose writings are Holy Ghost breathings that unveil consistent streams of fresh revelations straight from the Throne Room of Heaven. He is the president, founder and vision bearer of Frequency Revelator Ministries (FRM), a worldwide multiracial ministry that encompasses a myriad of movements with divine visions such as Resurrection Embassy (*The Global Church*), Christ Resurrection Movement (CRM) (*a Global movement for raising the dead*), the Global Apostolic & Prophetic Network (GAP) (a *Network of apostles, prophets and fivefold ministers across the globe*), Revival For Southern Africa (REFOSA) (*a Regional power-packed vision for Southern Africa*) and the Global Destiny Publishing House (GDP) (*the Ministry's publishing company*). The primary vision of this global ministry is to propagate the resurrection power of Christ from the Throne Room of Heaven to the extreme ends of the world and to launch the world into the greater depths of the miraculous. It is for this reason that Frequency Revelator Ministries (FRM) drives divergent apostolic and prophetic ministry visions and spiritual programmes such as the Global School of Resurrection (GSR), Global Resurrection Centre (GRC), the Global Healing Centre (GHC), Global School of Miracles, Signs and Wonders (SMSW), Global School of Kingdom Millionaires (SKM), Global Campus Ministry as well as Resurrection Conferences, Seminars and Training Centers. To fulfil its global mandate of soul winning, the ministry spearheads the Heavens' Broadcasting Commission (HBC) on television, a strategic ministerial initiative that broadcasts ministry programmes via the Dead Raising Channel *(a.k.a Resurrection TV)* and other Christian Television networks around the world.

Presiding over a global network of apostolic and prophetic visions, Apostle Frequency Revelator considers universities, colleges, high schools and other centers of learning as critical in fulfilling God's purpose and reaching the world for Christ, especially in this end-time season. As a Signs and Wonders Movement, the ministry hosts training sessions at the Global School of Resurrection (GSR) which includes but not limited to, impartation and activation of the gifts of the Spirit, prophetic declaration and ministration, invocations of open visions, angelic encounters and Throne Room visitations, revelational teachings, coaching and mentorship as well as Holy Ghost ministerial training sessions on how to practically raise the dead. This global ministry is therefore characterized by a deep revelation of God's word accompanied by a practical demonstration of God's power through miracles, signs and wonders manifested in raising cripples from wheel chairs, opening the eyes of the blind, unlocking the speech of the dumb, blasting off the ears of the deaf and raising the dead, as a manifestation of the finished works of the cross by the Lord Jesus Christ. The ministry is also punctuated with a plethora of manifestations of the wealth of Heaven through miracle money, coupled with the golden rain of gold dust, silver stones, supernatural oil and a torrent of creative miracles such as the development of the original blue print of body parts on bodily territories where they previously did not exist, germination of hair on bald heads, weight loss and gain, as well as instantaneous healings from HIV/AIDS, cancer, diabetes and every manner of sickness and disease which doctors have declared as incurable.

The author has written a collection of 21 anointed books, which include *The Realm of Power to Raise the Dead, How to become a Kingdom Millionaire, Deeper Revelations of The Anointing, Practical Demonstrations of The Anointing, How to Operate in the Realm of the Miraculous, The Realm of Glory, Unveiling the Mystery of Miracle Money, New Revelations of Faith, A Divine Revelation of the Supernatural Realm, The Prophetic Move of the Holy Spirit in the Contemporary Global Arena, The Ministry of Angels in the World Today, Kingdom Spiritual Laws and Principles, Divine Rights and Privileges of a Believer, Keys to Unlocking the Supernatural, The Prophetic Dimension, The Dynamics of God's Word, The Practice of God's Presence, Times of Refreshing and Restoration, The Power of Praying in the Throne Room, The End Time Revelations of Jesus Christ and Rain of Revelations,* which is a daily devotional concordance comprising a yearly record of 365 fresh revelations straight from the Throne Room of God.

Apostle Frequency Revelator resides in South Africa and he is a graduate of Fort Hare University, where his ministry took off. However, as a global minister, his ministry incorporates prophecy, deliverance and miracle healing crusades in the United Kingdom (UK), Southern Africa, India, Australia, USA, Canada and a dense network of ministry visions that covers the rest of the world. As a custodian of God's resurrection power, the apostle has been given a divine mandate from Heaven to raise a new breed of Apostles, Prophets, Pastors, Evangelists, Teachers, Kingdom Millionaires and Miracle Workers (*Dead raisers*) who shall propagate the world with the gospel of the Lord Jesus Christ and practically demonstrate His resurrection power through miracles, signs and wonders manifested in raising people from the dead, thereby launching the world in to the greater depths of the miraculous. To that effect, a conducive platform is therefore enacted for global impartation, mentorship, training and equipping ministers of the gospel for the work of ministry. Notable is the realization that the ministry ushers a new wave of signs and wonders that catapults the Body of Christ into higher realms of glory in which raising the dead is a common occurrence and demonstrating the viscosity of the glory of God in a visible and tangible manner is the order of the day. Having been mightily used by God to raise the dead, in this book, Apostle Frequency Revelator presents a practical model of how one can tap into the realm of God's resurrection power to raise the dead, impact the nations of the world and usher an unprecedented avalanche of billions of souls into the Kingdom, Glory to Jesus! May His Name be gloried, praised and honored forever more!

AUTHOR'S CONTACT INFORMATION

To know more about the ministry of Apostle Frequency Revelator, his publications, revelational teachings, global seminars, ministry schools, ministry products and Global missions, contact:

Apostle Frequency Revelator

@ Resurrection Embassy

(The Global Church)

Powered by Christ Resurrection Movement (CRM)

(Contact us in South Africa, United Kingdom, USA, Germany, Canada, Australia, India, Holland & Other nations of the world).

As a Global Vision, The Ministry of Apostle Frequency Revelator is present in all the continents of the World. You may contact us from any part of the world so that we can refer you to the Resident Ministry Pastors and Associates in respective nations.

Our offices and those of the ministry's publishing company (Global Destiny Publishing House (GDP House), are ready to dispatch any books requested from any part of the world.

Email:
frequency.revelator@gmail.com

Cell phone:

+27622436745

+27797921646/ +27785416006

Website:
www.globaldestinypublishers.co.za

Social Media Contacts:

The Author is also accessible on Social media via Facebook, twitter, instagram, YouTube, and other latest forms of social networks, as Apostle Frequency Revelator. For direct communication with the Apostle, you may invite him on Facebook and read his daily posts. You may also watch Apostle Frequency Revelator on the Dead Raising Channel a.k.a Resurrection TV and other Christian Television channels in your area.

Christian products:

You may also purchase DVDs, CDs, MP3s and possibly order all of the 21 anointed books published by Apostle Frequency Revelator, either as hard cover books or e-books. E-books are available on amazon.com, Baines & Nobles, create space, Kalahari.net and other e-book sites. You may also buy them directly from the author@ www.gdphouse.co.za. You may also request a collection of all powerful, revelational teachings by Apostle Frequency Revelator and we will promptly deliver them to you.

Ministry Networks & Partnerships:

If you want to partner with Apostle Frequency Revelator in executing this Global vision, partnership is available through divergent apostolic and prophetic ministry visions and spiritual programmes such as the Global School of Resurrection (GSR), Christ Resurrection Movement (CRM), Resurrection TV (a.k.a The Dead Raising Channel), the Global Apostolic & Prophetic Network (GAP), Global Resurrection Centre (GRC), the Global Healing Centre (GHC), Global School of Miracles, Signs and Wonders (SMSW), School of Kingdom Millionaires (SKM), Global Campus Ministry and other avenues. By partnering with Apostle Frequency Revelator, you are in a way joining hands with God's vision and thus setting yourself up for a life of increase, acceleration and superabundance.

ABOUT THE AUTHOR GLOBAL MISSIONS, PARTNERSHIPS & COLLABORATIONS:

If it happens that you are catapulted into a higher realm understanding divergent spiritual laws and principles of the kingdom following the reading of this book, please share your testimony with Apostle Frequency Revelator at the contacts above, so that you can strengthen other believers' faith in God all around the world. Your testimony will also be included in the next edition of this book.

If you want to invite Apostle Frequency Revelator to your church, city or community to come and spearhead Resurrection Seminars, Conferences, Dead Raising Training Sessions or conduct a Global School of Resurrection (GSR), whether in (Europe, Australia, Canada, USA, South America, Asia or Africa), you are welcome to do so.

If you want to start a Resurrection Centre or establish the Global School of Resurrection (GSR) in your church, city or community under this movement, you are also welcome to do so. We will be more than willing to send Copies of this book to whichever continent you live.

If you want your church or ministry to be part of the Christ Resurrection Movement (CRM) and join the bandwagon of raising the dead all around the world, you are welcome to be part of this Heaven-ordained commission.

If you want more copies of this book so that you can use them in your church for seminars, teachings, conferences, cell groups and global distribution, please don't hesitate to contact Apostle Frequency Revelator so that he can send the copies to whichever continent you are. Upon completion of this book, you may also visit www.amazon.com and under the "Book Review Section," write a brief review, commenting on how this book has impacted your life. This is meant to encourage readership by other believers all around the world.

If you want to donate or give freely to advance this global vision, you may also do so via our ministry website (www.globaldestinypublishers.co.za) or contact us at the details provided above. If you need a spiritual covering, impartation or mentorship for your Church or ministry as led by the Holy Spirit, you are welcome to contact us and join the league of dead-raising pastors that we are already mentoring in all continents of the world.

If you have a burning message that you would like to share with the whole world and you would want Apostle Frequency Revelator to help you turn your divine ideas and revelations into script and publish your first book, don't hesitate to contact us and submit a draft of your manuscript at the Global Destiny Publishing House (www.globaldestinypublishers.co.za). We will thoroughly polish your script and turn it into an amazing book filled with Throne Room revelations that will impact millions across the globe, glory to Jesus!

The Lord Jesus Christ is coming back soon!

Made in the USA
Coppell, TX
02 December 2022